Pastor Sam has done it again. He reminds us that the infinite power of God is able to sustain you through the ever-changing and unimaginable circumstances of life. Every page in this book reminds the reader that God is our strength and an ever-present help in time of need.

—Doug Clay
General Superintendent, The General Council of the Assemblies of God

From Survive to Thrive—the best I have seen yet to bring meaning and purpose to the worldwide pandemic. He challenges the church to think beyond the challenge of the moment to the God's-eye view for the times we are in. Relevant is an understatement.

—Jentezen Franklin
Senior Pastor, Free Chapel
New York Times Best-Selling Author

From Survive to Thrive is an imperative book for this season. Dr. Sammy Rodriguez holds an influential position in the world today and not only provides incredible strategic insight but shares a prophetic worldview that will help you thrive in any season.

—Russell Evans
Senior Pastor, Planetshakers

In the midst of a global pandemic or any number of other challenges we face in life these days, *From Survive to Thrive* is a spiritual prescription for such a time as this. Using examples straight from Scripture, you will learn to reboot, recharge, and restart and even discover your true calling and destiny in the middle of life's most isolating and challenging moments. A highly engaging, highly encouraging read!

—Matthew Crouch
President, Trinity Broadcasting Network

Dreams often die when the culture is unfriendly to making them live. This is why I am thrilled to know that in the midst of one of the most difficult and strenuous times in history, Pastor Sam Rodriguez once again issues a compelling call to each of us to rise up in this moment and answer it with faith and hope. Thank you, Sam, for reminding us that nothing is impossible with God.

—Dr. Ronnie Floyd
President and CEO, Southern Baptist Convention
Executive Committee
Pastor Emeritus, Cross Church

With thousands of voices trying to distract us due to COVID-19, some have wandered away from the path of intimacy with God. In his new book, *From Survive to Thrive*, Pastor Samuel Rodriguez, with his keen insights into the Bible, powerful stories, and penetrating writing style, invites those who need a fresh touch of the Master's hand on a journey to renewed faith and hope. The Lord has given Pastor Sammy a voice of strength, comfort, and peace within the pages of this book. A must-read for all God's children who desire to *thrive* with a fresh fire of God's spirit and not just *survive*. This book is relevant, revelatory, and highly readable for the season we are living in. I highly recommend it!

—Marcus D. Lamb
Founder and President, Daystar Television Network

Sammy Rodriguez is an amazing guy. He is full of passion to reach people with the gospel. In his new book, *From Survive to Thrive*, he brings much-needed hope to people who find themselves burned-out and discouraged. This book will help you get out of mere survival mode and point you toward following God's purpose, which is to know Him and to make Him known.

—Greg Laurie
Senior Pastor, Harvest Christian Fellowship
Founder, Harvest Crusades

Pastor Samuel Rodriguez is a gift to the body of Christ. *From Survive to Thrive* is a *now* word for today's world and a timely reminder to the church that uncertainty and chaos are the backdrop against which the light of God in us shines brightest. Only God can flip the script to turn a difficult season into a divine one. This book will fuel you with hope and courage to see in and through every storm.

—PASTOR MARK VARUGHESE
FOUNDER AND SENIOR LEADER, KINGDOMCITY
AUTHOR, *READY FIRE! AIM*

From Survive to Thrive is water to thirsty souls. These chaotic, stressful days in which we live have left us parched, and this book brings much-needed refreshment. When our circumstances threaten to overwhelm us, these words reassure us that God sees us, knows us, and wants to bless us.

—PAULA WHITE CAIN
FOUNDER AND PRESIDENT, PAULA WHITE MINISTRIES
SPIRITUAL ADVISER TO PRESIDENT DONALD J. TRUMP
OVERSIGHT PASTOR, CITY OF DESTINY, APOPKA, FLORIDA
AUTHOR, *SOMETHING GREATER: FINDING
TRIUMPH OVER TRIALS*

Hope is such a beautiful thing; without it we are lost. Scripture says, "Hope deferred makes the heart sick" (Prov. 13:12). Sammy takes us on a dynamic ride to the true source of real hope and healing!

—DR. TIM CLINTON
PRESIDENT, AMERICAN ASSOCIATION OF
CHRISTIAN COUNSELORS
EXECUTIVE DIRECTOR, JAMES DOBSON FAMILY INSTITUTE

From Survive to Thrive offers us hope in a time when the world seems to have none. This book reminds us that our all-knowing, all-present, and all-powerful God is with us in our suffering and distress, even if we can't discern how He is working.

—Dr. Tony Evans
President, The Urban Alternative
Senior Pastor, Oak Cliff Bible Fellowship

Rev. Samuel Rodriguez is one of the most important religious leaders in the world. Read everything he writes.

—Rev. Johnnie Moore
President, Congress of Christian Leaders

We are living through hard times. Everywhere we turn, we see a world filled with anxiety, fear, worry, and depression—but even when our circumstances look impossible, my friend Sam Rodriguez reminds us that God is at work and our Good Shepherd will lead us through the dark valley to green pastures and still waters. If you are looking for hope during trying times, read this book.

—Dr. Jack Graham
Pastor, Prestonwood Baptist Church
Founder, PowerPoint Ministries

From SURVIVE to THRIVE

From SURVIVE to THRIVE

SAMUEL RODRIGUEZ

CHARISMA HOUSE

Most CHARISMA HOUSE BOOK GROUP products are available at special quantity discounts for bulk purchase for sales promotions, premiums, fund-raising, and educational needs. For details, call us at (407) 333-0600 or visit our website at www.charismahouse.com.

FROM SURVIVE TO THRIVE by Samuel Rodriguez
Published by Charisma House
Charisma Media/Charisma House Book Group
600 Rinehart Road, Lake Mary, Florida 32746

Copyright © 2020 by Samuel Rodriguez
All rights reserved

Visit the author's website at PastorSam.com,
www.SamuelRodriguezBooks.com.

Library of Congress Cataloging-in-Publication Data:
An application to register this book for cataloging has been submitted to the Library of Congress.
International Standard Book Number: 978-1-62999-840-4
E-book ISBN: 978-1-62999-841-1

20 21 22 23 24 — 9 8 7 6 5 4 3 2 1
Printed in the United States of America

*I dedicate this book to our
eldest daughter, Yvonne. You survived
life's valleys, including COVID-19 (ICU), and
you refused to just survive; you thrived!
Your father loves you.*

Contents

Acknowledgments

I am grateful for a group of thrivers who reject failure and refuse to just survive. My thrive team: Eva Rodriguez, Nathan Rodriguez, Lauren Rodriguez, Dudley Deffs, Ned Clements, Tony Suarez, Gus Reyes, Armando Martinez, Nick Garza, Mercedes Ray, Jeff Carter, Girien Salazar, April Barnes, Charlie Rivera, Monica Kirkland, and Ditmores. Without these people, this book would not be the tool it is to help its readers not just survive but thrive!

Chapter 1

SOUL SURVIVOR—SHELTER IN PLACE

*When you can't imagine how you will survive,
take shelter where you are and trust God.*

*He will find you when others overlook you
and calamity stands in your way.*

OUR WORLD CHANGED overnight.

In a matter of days into weeks, the COVID-19 pandemic engulfed the globe, bringing dramatic changes to virtually every area of our lives. Like wildfire spreading from a distant wilderness into our own backyards, the novel coronavirus attacked human bodies regardless of age, gender, race, income, education, or status. While the elderly and infirm seemed most susceptible, the virus defied categories and seemingly attacked arbitrarily. Accurate information on its transmission, incubation, and rate of contagion could not be pinned down.

Because it was a new virus, science reached its limitations quickly and found it difficult to discern accurate patterns of how it spread, who was most susceptible, and what we could do to protect ourselves and our families. Government and civic leaders struggled to know the best course of action to prevent the spread of the disease. Painful divisions fractured into battle lines. We weren't sure who to trust and what to believe.

As businesses at every level, large and small, adjusted to prohibit and contain the virus, the national and global economies dropped to record historic lows. Millions lost their jobs. International travel ceased as numerous countries closed their borders and airlines suspended flights. Even domestic travel crawled to a standstill as people self-quarantined and those blessed to retain employment worked from home. Schools and universities closed and instead turned to online learning.

Before I could even finish completing this chapter, each day brought dire news of closures, chaos, and confusion as the contagion spread, infecting an unknown number of people and claiming the lives of thousands. We learned what it means to shelter in place, to practice social distancing, and to stock up on toilet paper! The repercussions continue and likely will for years to come.

Even in the bleakest, most overwhelming days of the pandemic, however, we never lost hope. We know the battle belongs to the Lord and that He is the source of all healing. Out of this humbling, crippling experience, followers of Jesus have discovered new opportunities for relying on God's power to sustain us through unimaginable circumstances even as He uses us to do the impossible. We know that Christ died to heal you and me and everyone suffering—physically, emotionally, mentally, spiritually, relationally, financially, and beyond. God's Word could not be clearer: "But he was pierced for our rebellion, crushed for our sins. He was beaten so we could be whole. He was whipped so we could be healed" (Isa. 53:5, NLT).

Jesus conquered the power of sin and death in our lives once and for all, becoming the perfect sacrifice to pay a debt none of us could fulfill. "He himself carried our sins in his body on the cross so that we would be dead to sin and live for righteousness," we're told. "Our instant healing flowed from his wounding" (1 Pet. 2:24, TPT). Even before Christ came to earth in human form, God's people knew of His healing touch: "He heals the brokenhearted and binds up their wounds" (Ps. 147:3).

No matter what you're going through, no matter how you're suffering, no matter what you've lost, nothing—not even the coronavirus—can prevent you from knowing the healing touch of the Great Physician! God has not brought you this far and sustained you through the worst of the worldwide pandemic so you can merely survive. He has not blessed you and equipped you so that you can merely return to the status quo. Drawing on the promises of God's Word and the power of His Holy Spirit, you can stop scrambling to survive and experience the divine anointing to thrive!

POINT OF IMPACT

No human being healthy in mind, body, and spirit enjoys pain. By its very definition pain causes distress, disruption, and dysfunction. Whether acute with the sharp intensity of a blade stabbing through your body or chronic with the dull, unbearable ambience of constant paper cuts, pain directs our attention to the location of our wounding. If someone comes up and punches you, then you become aware of the point of impact and the resulting pain on contact. Your jaw receives the force of the fist pummeling your face. Instinctively you turn to avoid the blow to your nose, eyes, or temple in an attempt to protect the most sensitive areas prone to the most damage. Nerve endings transmit pain back to your brain as your body instantly begins to assess the damage and initiate recovery.

The coronavirus, its devastating economic impact, and all the unrest and turmoil our nation and our world has faced has left all of us reeling in the agony of a comprehensive assault. The uncertainty of its approach, the duration of its attack, and its uncompromising assassination of hope left us gasping in ways few people alive in the world today have ever experienced. Leaders we trusted seemed to know less than we did. Organizations and institutions disintegrated into anarchies and oligarchies. As we wondered how we would pay our bills and provide for our families, we felt orphaned and isolated, left without resources in a world depleted and exhausted.

For all of their crushing destruction and lingering effects, the circumstances of the recent past have an eternally significant silver lining: *We have nowhere to run except to God.*

When times are good and our families are healthy and our jobs secure, when we're enjoying an abundance of God's blessings to the point that we've come to feel entitled to them, when we slip into old ways of thinking that we can control our lives, there's only one way to get our attention. Because when we lose something or someone, when the future we had mapped out suddenly vanishes in a matter of minutes, then we realize just how little control we have over anything in our lives. We recognize our limitations in these mortal bodies and turn back to the omniscient, all-powerful almighty God, Creator of heaven and earth.

The temptation during such trials might be to despair and wonder why we have to suffer while it appears others do not. Like Job, a man whom God allowed to lose everything—his family, his fortune, his health—we cannot fathom what we have done to deserve such anguish and suffer such loss. But when the whole world is suffering alongside us—when we look around at our friends and neighbors, our coworkers and colleagues, our acquaintances and familiar faces, and see the smoldering pain and vacant expressions—it can be even more confusing. When we're unable to embrace loved ones and forced to endure unbearable distances apart with no end in sight, we feel confined by our loneliness.

We may even be tempted to rage against God and cast blame on Him for allowing us to suffer so harshly for so long. Or we may erroneously assume He caused such devastation in our lives when we know it is in His power to protect us. This is when we must remember that God never promised us a life of safety and comfort but a life of transformation. We often become so committed to avoiding pain of any kind in our lives that we lose sight of its fundamental function: to allow God's works to be displayed.

PRISM OF PAIN

When we endure trials on the scale of the global pandemic, we must resist the temptation to play the blame game. These lines of thinking are natural and reactive and usually cannot be avoided in the midst of such calamity. Anytime something goes wrong or we suffer a loss, we're likely to wonder why. Jesus' disciples even posed this question once when they encountered a man who had been blind since birth:

> "Rabbi, who sinned, this man or his parents, that he was born blind?"
> "Neither this man nor his parents sinned," said Jesus, "but this happened so that the works of God might be displayed in him. As long as it is day, we must do the works of him who sent me. Night is coming, when no one can work. While I am in the world, I am the light of the world."
> After saying this, he spit on the ground, made some mud with the saliva, and put it on the man's eyes. "Go," he told him, "wash in the Pool of Siloam" (this word means "Sent"). So the man went and washed, and came home seeing.
> —JOHN 9:2–7

Our trials can become opportunities for God's light to shine through the cracks of our brokenness. God's glory pours forth into the hard, raw places of our lives and provides a poultice to soothe our wounds and restore our hope. Out of the muddy mess of dirt and saliva Jesus reveals the power to heal and cleanse. Rather than blame this man's sin or his parents or God for making him blind, Jesus gave this man more than just the gift of sight; he became a living testament to the way God turns trials into triumphs.

If we want to transcend our goal to survive in order to thrive, then we must be willing to see by faith rather than by the sensory data viewed by our human eyes. We must allow our gritty circumstances to become the raw material for the masterpiece God wants to shape so that we can serve as His holy vessel. Rather than seeking to escape our pain, we can allow it to redirect our attention to a greater opportunity to trust God with every aspect of our well-being. As C. S. Lewis wrote, "Pain insists upon being attended to. God whispers to us in our pleasures, speaks in our conscience, but shouts in our pains: it is His megaphone to rouse a deaf world."[1]

Right now, you are reading this book for a reason. God wants you to know He has not forgotten you and your needs. Your Creator has carried you through the unimaginable trials of recent times in order to strengthen you, empower you, and redirect your attention to what matters most. Through the power of Christ in you, you are not merely a survivor but a conqueror. In fact, God's Word tells us we are *more* than conquerors (Rom. 8:37). Nothing can separate you from the love of God and the power of His Spirit in you! "If God is for us, who can be against us?...For I am convinced that neither death nor life, neither angels nor demons, neither the present nor the future, nor any powers, neither height nor depth, nor anything else in all creation, will be able to separate us from the love of God that is in Christ Jesus our Lord" (Rom. 8:31, 38–39).

God wants to use your pain as a prism for His glory.

UNEXPECTED ANOINTING

As insurmountable, overwhelming, and undermining as the pandemic and its collateral damage may seem to us, we are not the first to face impossible life-or-death challenges. We're not the first to be told by experts and authority figures that there's no way for us to recover and survive, let alone to endure and thrive. We're not the only people to place our trust in God while others roll their eyes and pity us for what they consider to be naïve, misplaced hope in the unimaginable. The Bible is filled with champions of the faith who dared to believe rather than despair, who endured trials until they tasted triumph, who walked on water and faced the fire, who parted the sea and survived a flood, who wrestled angels and defeated armies.

One such champion lived a life of defying the odds and overcoming the impossible. His life provides a field guide for not merely surviving but thriving. One of his greatest challenges in particular fascinates me and serves as the inspiration for this book. Even before he arrived at the moment when he faced a showdown with the insidious force waging war against him and his people, this young man had to overcome the doubts, desperation, and denigration of those he sought to protect and redeem. They were reluctant to allow him to step out in faith without anything other than the will to survive and God's anointing on him to thrive.

This young man's name was David, the renowned shepherd boy, harp player, and psalmist and the youngest son of Jesse, with eight older brothers. He first entered the picture when King Saul ruled over Israel, even as Saul began turning away from God and His divine direction for His chosen people. God knew it was time to move on and select the next king even before Saul's reign had officially ended. So God lit the mortal fuse to ignite young David's divine destiny:

The LORD said to Samuel, "How long will you mourn for Saul, since I have rejected him as king over Israel? Fill your horn with oil and be on your way; I am sending you to Jesse of Bethlehem. I have chosen one of his sons to be king."

But Samuel said, "How can I go? If Saul hears about it, he will kill me."

The LORD said, "Take a heifer with you and say, 'I have come to sacrifice to the LORD.' Invite Jesse to the sacrifice, and I will show you what to do. You are to anoint for me the one I indicate."

Samuel did what the LORD said. When he arrived at Bethlehem, the elders of the town trembled when they met him. They asked, "Do you come in peace?"

Samuel replied, "Yes, in peace; I have come to sacrifice to the LORD. Consecrate yourselves and come to the sacrifice with me." Then he consecrated Jesse and his sons and invited them to the sacrifice.

When they arrived, Samuel saw Eliab and thought, "Surely the LORD's anointed stands here before the LORD."

But the LORD said to Samuel, "Do not consider his appearance or his height, for I have rejected him. The LORD does not look at the things people look at. People look at the outward appearance, but the LORD looks at the heart."

—1 SAMUEL 16:1–7

Notice how Samuel, God's prophet and royal ambassador, immediately thinks of the obstacle to obeying the Lord's instructions. Apparently Samuel was as human as the rest of us and looked ahead at the possible worst-case scenario, being executed by an angry king who found out the prophet was looking for a royal replacement. Remember, too, that Samuel was not a novice in his relationship with God, which is perhaps a bit reassuring if you have doubts or tend to automatically imagine the worst that can happen.

No matter how long we've been walking with God, it's still tempting to focus on the cost of our obedience and find a reason we can't pay that price. After all I've seen God do in my life and all the walls I've walked through where He has opened a door for me, I'm prone to look for landmines in the path I'm called to follow, as if God doesn't know they're there and must rely on me to disable them. When God calls us for His purposes, we don't have to worry about how we'll get there or what it will take to make a way. We can take shelter in His promises.

In Samuel's case, God shared His plan for the prophet to drop in on the household of a man named Jesse, who lived in Bethlehem with his eight sons, one of whom was apparently the next king of Israel. As a cover story to circumvent Saul, Samuel was told to make a sacrifice near Jesse's house and invite the family to join him. This would allow Samuel to anoint the young man God would reveal to him. Following human logic, the prophet noticed the oldest, Eliab, and assumed he must be the one, only to be informed that God's selection criteria are not based on appearances.

Eliab was a likely candidate and may have looked the part of what Samuel assumed a king should look like. Maybe he was tall and strong, rugged and attractive, asserting confidence and charisma to the people around him. It didn't matter, though. God made that loud and clear to Samuel, basically saying, "Look, I'm not choosing who you think I will. I don't use the same basis that people use. They go by how someone looks, and first impressions. But I go much deeper than that—I look at someone's heart."

Maybe you've made the same mistake Samuel made and assumed something about another person only to be proven wrong. Maybe your first impression, based solely on your five senses, turned out to be an inaccurate indicator of who this person really was and what they were about. Perhaps you've even been in this position yourself and had others assume things about you, either positive or negative but more likely something critical, based on how you look, what you're wearing, your perceived age, the sound of your voice, your accent, your mannerisms, the color of your skin, the smell of your cologne— or lack of!

Thank goodness, though, you and I are more than the details of our appearances. No matter how we think we look or how others see us, God knows what's inside us, in our hearts, and that's what matters. If you've opened your heart to Him, if you're willing to follow Jesus and be led by His Holy Spirit, then it doesn't matter how others see you. You are God's chosen one! You are a precious daughter or son of the King of kings and a royal heir with Christ. Others often base their conclusions about you on external details, but God peers into who you really are—His holy creation, made in His image, redeemed by His Son, and filled with His Spirit.

A SACRED SEARCH

Even after God told Samuel not to rely on how Jesse's sons looked, the old prophet kept going down the line according to age, which reflected the cultural custom of honoring the firstborn male and graduating down from there. Once again, though, God wasn't relying on cultural customs. Notice that the person God had selected to be His next king of Israel was the one overlooked and disregarded by everyone else:

> Then Jesse called Abinadab and had him pass in front of Samuel. But Samuel said, "The LORD has not chosen this one either." Jesse then had Shammah pass by, but Samuel said, "Nor has the LORD chosen this one." Jesse had seven

of his sons pass before Samuel, but Samuel said to him, "The LORD has not chosen these." So he asked Jesse, "Are these all the sons you have?"

"There is still the youngest," Jesse answered. "He is tending the sheep."

Samuel said, "Send for him; we will not sit down until he arrives."

So he sent for him and had him brought in. He was glowing with health and had a fine appearance and handsome features.

Then the LORD said, "Rise and anoint him; this is the one."

So Samuel took the horn of oil and anointed him in the presence of his brothers, and from that day on the Spirit of the LORD came powerfully upon David.

—1 SAMUEL 16:8–13

You wonder if Samuel was scratching his head here and wondering what was going on! It's like a holy game of hot potato, with the prophet thinking he must be getting warmer to the person God has chosen, but one after another he couldn't find the subject of his sacred search. Assuming there had to be another, Samuel had Jesse send for his youngest, his baby boy out tending the sheep in the nearby pastures.

When Jesse overlooked David from his visitor's consideration, this dad probably wasn't casting intentional shade or criticism toward his youngest son. As Jesse may have seen it— again, relying on human appearances and logic—David simply seemed irrelevant to Samuel's quest. The idea of someone so young, so untested, so naïve and inexperienced chosen by God to be king? You must be joking!

While we're not told how old David was at this time, many Bible scholars and historians speculate he was probably somewhere between ten and fifteen, a tween or young adolescent. It's curious in the details we're given here, too, that David was "glowing with health and had a fine appearance and handsome features" (1 Sam. 16:12). In other words, this good-looking young man did look like a future king by human standards, at least objectively. Based on this kind of description, David could be the prince or royal heir in any Disney movie.

Perhaps seeing that young David was such a handsome lad made it easier for Samuel to accept God's revelation, "This is the one" (1 Sam. 16:12). Regardless, Samuel knew better than to question God's selection by this point—after all, there were no other candidates left in the household! So the prophet obeyed the Lord's instruction and anointed David in the presence of his family, "and from that day on the Spirit of the LORD came powerfully upon David" (1 Sam. 16:13).

There's no mention of David's reaction to this news other than accepting what has been asked of him. Based on some of the poetic songs David wrote, both for God and to God, and collected in our Book of Psalms, it seems reasonable to conclude this young shepherd boy enjoyed a remarkable closeness with the Lord. This deduction is confirmed by the fact that David is described not once but twice in the pages of Scripture as "a man after God's own heart." (See 1 Samuel 13:14 and Acts 13:22.)

When God sent His prophet Samuel to find and anoint God's next king of Israel, everyone overlooked David at first. As the youngest, he wasn't even considered a grown man yet, let alone experienced enough to prove himself worthy of being the leader of God's chosen people. He was just a kid and knew nothing of palace life or political issues. He had never served in the military because most young men were at least twenty when they joined. He had not been trained by rabbis in the temple about God's Law and the sacred Scriptures.

Despite his youth and inexperience, though, David had what it takes. God knew David's heart, that it was open and soft, tender and receptive to the things of God. If you're willing to open yourself to God, to follow Him, trust Him, serve Him, and be led by Him, then you, too, can be someone after God's own heart—no matter what others say or when you've been overlooked. Despite all that you may have lost or suffered this past year, you still have a choice to trust God, to believe that your soul survival is part of His plan for your life.

A GIANT NO

David didn't have to wait long to be tested. While the chronology isn't specified, this giant showdown likely came after David had been anointed by Samuel. We know David was still at home in Bethlehem shepherding sheep for his father and that David's three oldest brothers—Eliab, Abinadab, and Shammah—were soldiers in Saul's army (1 Sam. 17:13) because Jesse sends David to the battlefront with food and provisions for them (1 Sam. 17:17–19).

When David arrives at the army encampment, the scene is grim. Saul and his men are basically in a standoff with the Philistines, with their army encamped on one hill and their opponents on the next hill with only a valley between them. It's not looking good for the home team. In fact, we're told Saul and all the Israelites were "dismayed and terrified" (1 Sam. 17:11) after being taunted by a rival champion named Goliath who would put any current WWE superstar wrestler to shame. We're given great detail about Goliath's height—just under ten feet—the weight of his elaborate bronze armor and weaponry— about 150 pounds—and the fact that he loved being a bully (1 Sam. 17:4–10). This dude loved playing the villain, a lifelong soldier who commanded attention and respect because of his sheer size.

Every day for forty days Goliath sneered at the Israelites and baited them. He loved messing with their minds and preparing for what he assumed would be the blood sport of decimating any and all of them. The giant had them exactly where he wanted them: afraid and desperate, and probably a little ashamed as well that none of them had the courage to accept the Philistine's challenge and go face to face with him.

Then David showed up and annoyed everybody he encountered—his brothers, Saul, and especially Goliath—with his faith-fueled confidence. David's big brother Eliab told him, "I know how conceited you are and how wicked your heart is; you came down only to watch the battle" (1 Sam. 17:28). Ouch—talk about sibling rivalry!

Eliab made the same mistake many people make when they see the holy confidence and bold faith within you: he interpreted David's courage as conceit and his obedience as ego. When you are chosen, anointed, and empowered by God, you will make other people uncomfortable. They may not know what to do with you and so assume you have a self-serving agenda. They can't grasp what it means to be filled with God's Spirit to the point where you banish fear and step out in faith no matter how great the odds against you. They had rather believe you are arrogant instead of anointed, cocky rather than chosen, and self-serving instead of sold out to your Savior!

David didn't let his big bro's harsh, accusatory words deter his drive to defeat the disgrace of allowing their enemy to mock them—and worse still, mock the living God. Word of David's intention to square off with Goliath and redeem Israel and honor God made its way back to Saul, who sent for this young man who was either incredibly brave or incredibly foolish. The simple purity of David's determination must have seemed absurd if not pathetic when David told Saul, "Don't worry about this Philistine...I'll go fight him!" (1 Sam. 17:32, NLT).

The king wasted no time responding to David's offer: "Don't be ridiculous! There's no way you can fight this Philistine and possibly win! You're only a boy, and he's been a man of war since his youth" (1 Sam. 17:33, NLT).

In no uncertain terms, David was told no.

TAKE SHELTER IN GOD'S YES

David was explicitly told it would not happen. He was denied even the opportunity to fulfill his offer. He would not be given his shot.

When have you been told no? When have you been told that it was impossible? When have you been told not to waste your time trying? When has your shot been denied? When have you experienced the same incredulous ridicule that mighty King Saul expressed to a young shepherd boy centuries ago? When have others mocked you for trusting God to provide for all your needs during the pandemic?

From my experience, this kind of friction happens every day. We offer to serve and do what we can for others only to be denied the opportunity, dismissed, and shamed for daring to try. I can relate to that sense of astonishment of being denied an opportunity. I can identify with the righteous outrage David may have felt momentarily when he heard his courageous, faith-fueled offer trampled by the one able to authorize it.

At an early age I was told by a school guidance counselor that I could not pursue my educational dreams. Although I was just as American as any other US citizen born in Pennsylvania, I faced assumptions based on appearances. Seeing I was of Puerto Rican descent, my guidance counselor gave me her most patronizing expression and said, "Have you thought about gardening? Or a service job? Are you taking advantage of our school's vocational training courses?"

When I pointed out that I was taking advanced classes for

college-bound students, her expression conveyed the same weight as Saul's words to David: *"Don't be ridiculous!"* She told me my aspirations were "unrealistic," but her message was unmistakable: Who did I think I was, talking about my high grade-point average, college-prep courses, and applications for scholarships? Didn't I know my place? Didn't I know that people like me aren't allowed to dream and seize the opportunities given to them?

By the grace of God and my loving, supportive family I persevered, continued working hard, and let my testimony reveal God's desire for me to thrive. When I was told no, I took shelter in God's yes.

That was the first of many times I've been told no. The Sauls of my generation told me as often as possible, "Don't be ridiculous, Samuel!" At best they viewed my dreams of starting an organization that reconciled Billy Graham's gospel message with Dr. Martin Luther King Jr.'s march for justice as naïve. Yet here we are, twenty years later, by the grace of God and for the glory of His name, as I lead an organization with more than 42,000 certified member churches, making it one of the largest Christian organizations on the planet!

> *I haven't merely survived—by the power of God and for His glory, I have thrived!*

When I was young, God spoke to me through other people as well as through His Spirit and told me to be prepared because one day I would have access to the White House, that I would be leading and serving alongside some of the most powerful and influential people in the world for the purpose of advancing the Lamb's agenda. Whenever I shared this prophetic awareness, I was scorned, derided, and rebuked. I was asked, "Why would anyone grant you access to the corridors of national and international power?" Yet here for the glory of

Jesus I have been advising three presidents of the United States of America in addition to influential leaders from around the globe.

Approximately a decade ago God gave me a word regarding Hollywood. I wondered what He was up to but obediently followed His direction toward the film industry. Anytime others noticed this direction I was taking, they would respond, "Really? You? This Hispanic American Evangelical leader producing movies—real movies released in theaters across the country and around the world—in Hollywood? Never! Don't make me laugh!" As I write this book, I am filled with praise to God for the privilege of serving as executive producer of the hit film *Breakthrough*. Along with 20th Century Fox, I partnered to bring *Breakthrough*'s uplifting inspirational message to countless viewers, and it has now emerged as Inspirational Film of the Year at the Dove Awards and received an Oscar nomination for best original song.

I'm humbled, astounded, and exhilarated by all that God has done and continues to do through my efforts to serve Him and His kingdom. By His grace alone and for the glory of His name I am the first Hispanic American Evangelical to advise three US presidents, the first Latino Evangelical producer of a major motion picture, and the first person in my ethnic group as well as my denomination to ever participate in a presidential inauguration before hundreds of millions of people watching around the world. I can express with the fear of God in a humble spirit that in Christ all things are possible.

> *By the grace of God I have continually moved from survive to thrive!*

I completely understand that absolutely everything that I have that is good comes from above. I am wholeheartedly aware that all my blessings flow from the throne room of grace. I am not naïve to the fact that every door, every opportunity, every breakthrough emerges out of the grace-filled vicarious atoning work of Jesus in me, with me, and through me. I am living proof that by the grace of God I am what I am (1 Cor. 15:10).

Yet even as I share with you these unprecedented victories in my life, I am filled with hope and faith that as you read this book, you can push back on every single naysayer, detractor, hater, obstacle, hindrance, impediment, obstruction, lie of the enemy, doubt, shame, condemnation, toxic trial, self-pity party, and victimization mindset. No matter what or where or who is the source attempting to deny you the unlimited adventure of what it means to thrive, they are mistaken. Whether kindly intended, spitefully said, or onerously offered, they know nothing of who you are and what God has for you.

I have full confidence that this is your season to slay your giant. This is your season, your hour, your moment to rise up and by faith in the name of Jesus, empowered by His precious Holy Spirit with unprecedented humility and grace, declare, "I will survive in order to thrive!"

ALIVE TO THRIVE

Closing out each chapter, you will find a few questions to help you reflect on my message and apply it to your own life. This isn't homework, and you don't have to write down your responses, but you might be surprised to discover how helpful it can be to keep a record of how God speaks to you through these pages. After you've spent a few moments thinking about your answers to these questions, I encourage you to go to the Lord in prayer and share with Him what's going on in your heart. To help you get started, you'll find a short prayer to begin your conversation with Him, the One who loves you most, your Father who delights in empowering you when you're willing to step out in faith and thrive!

1. When has God selected you to carry out His purposes despite your lack of qualifications, experience, or human abilities? How did you feel as you answered His call? How did others respond as you stepped forward in obedient faith?

2. What does the word *hero* mean to you? Who are some heroes of the faith or role models you admire or aspire to be like? What is it about them you want to emulate? Why?

3. What obstacles stand in the way of the limitless life God has for you? Which ones have been removed by God already? What's the biggest barrier as you transition from surviving to thriving?

Dear God, I sometimes give in to doubt when others put me down or tell me why I can't do what I know You've called me to do. Bolster my faith in You and Your goodness. Give me the strength to respond to them with the same strength, acceptance, and grace that David displayed when even the king told him that he could never defeat Goliath. Help me to be resourceful, resilient, and reliant on Your power alone to do what appears impossible by human standards. I trust You, Lord, and surrender my pride, my feelings, my fear, and any resistance within me. My confidence comes from You and You alone! Amen.

Chapter 2

HOLY QUARANTINE—REBOOT, RECHARGE, RESTART

When we face giant obstacles in life,
we must go back to basics and rely on God.

He has already provided what we need
not simply to survive but to thrive!

THE SPREAD OF the COVID-19 virus required all of us to be quarantined. This global pandemic necessitated all of us to live, at least for a season, behind closed doors. Removed from the rest of society, including our extended families, friends, and communities, we isolated ourselves to stop the transmission of the deadly disease. This way, those who had the virus but were asymptomatic would not unknowingly pass it on to others equally unaware. Healthy people would also remain virus-free without human interaction in gathering places and hot spots where COVID-19 seemed especially active and deadly.

Sheltering in place became a ubiquitous phrase catapulted into mainstream usage. While it does not convey the stringent, clinical boundaries carried by the word *quarantine*, I suspect its impact was similar nonetheless. People were separated for their own protection and the well-being of the population at large.

This commonsense concept dates back centuries. When the bubonic plague swept through Europe during the fourteenth century, Italian officials controlling port cities passed laws requiring sailors to endure a thirty-day period of isolation without symptoms before they entered the city. Known as *trentino*, from the Italian word for *thirty*, this sequestering prevented local visitors from boarding the ships as well. As this practice began to yield positive results and impede the contagion of the Black Death, as it was known, other cities and communities adopted it as well. Somewhere along the way the period of isolation was extended to forty days, perhaps just to be on the safe side, which was called *quarantino*, the genesis of our word *quarantine*.[1]

During the novel coronavirus pandemic, our isolation forced us to alter every aspect of our lifestyle: working, shopping, meeting, eating, worshipping, and communicating. Graduates from the class of 2020 accepted the reality of virtual commencement ceremonies, unable to congregate and celebrate with classmates and faculty, family and friends. Survivors of loved ones who succumbed to the virus or other fatal agents grieved alone, compounding the sorrowful knowledge that so many people passed from this life alone as well.

For the rest of us in between such bittersweet milestones, each day seemed to flow into another with little distinction from weekdays to weekends. We stocked up on groceries, ordered household goods online, hoarded toilet paper, and Zoomed from home to attend work meetings and to see loved ones across the miles. We relied on social media more than ever to stay connected even as we often felt more isolated than ever before. We worshipped together online or sat in our cars in church parking lots and participated like viewers at drive-in movies, tuning in to praise music, testimonies, teaching, and preaching.

While we adapted, it was rarely easy. Many of us felt restricted, confined, caged by forces beyond our control, which made us automatically focus on only negative aspects of this quarantine. Only as busy schedules were reduced to more manageable speeds and overwhelming to-do lists became whittled down to essentials did we begin to see the benefits of such limitations. Suddenly we had more face-to-face time with our families as events, meetings, classes, sports, and concerts were cancelled or postponed indefinitely.

As the winter weeks of gray melted into the mild blue skies of spring, we ventured outdoors for walks, bike rides, reading on the porch, or playing with our children. Our priorities were reordered for us whether we liked it or not. Left to focus singularly on taking care of ourselves, our families, and each other, we looked for silver linings beyond the enforced restrictions.

What we found was a sense of *holy quarantine.*

BEHIND CLOSED DOORS

Prior to the pandemic we used to hear so much about open doors. Churches looked for ways to open doors for ministry, while businesses and schools implemented open-door policies. People would say, "I'm waiting for a door to open before I step out in faith. I know God's going to suddenly open doors in my favor. And once that door swings open, then I'll walk through it."

There's nothing wrong with this attitude. Most of the time, at least prior to the coronavirus, open doors signified a welcoming stance, an invitation of inclusivity, and a willingness to expand borders and boundaries. But when we limit ourselves to open doors, we overlook the opportunities afforded by being set apart. Relying on open doors, we minimize the beauty and blessing of what takes place behind closed doors.

Even the phrase *behind closed doors* often has an ominous

ring to it. Private meetings take place behind closed doors along with sketchy deals and illicit relationships. Personal conversations are kept behind closed doors when speakers want to protect their privacy and confidentiality. There's an assumed sense of enclosure and intimacy, exclusivity and separation, protection from prying eyes and listening ears.

We need not assume conspiracies, shady business dealings, and unethical practices are synonymous with *behind closed doors*, because sometimes we need the solitude, sanctuary, and stillness closed doors provide. "Be still, and know that I am God," the Bible tells us (Ps. 46:10). Miraculous, transformative, and holy things often take place behind closed doors. Only in the quiet tranquility of resting in the arms of God can we discover the depths of His love for us. Only behind closed doors can we experience the soothing balm of peace afforded by the Spirit's embrace.

Now more than ever we long for the security, assurance, and peace that passes understanding as we endure the ongoing shock waves of the pandemic and its economic and social trauma. Most of us have found our faith stretched and tested like never before. We want to trust God but find ourselves tempted by despair as the world as we have known it crumbles before our eyes. Anxiety and depression, already rampant in our chaotic world before the coronavirus, became twin children of the pandemic forever tugging at our minds, hearts, and souls. Without the support of others, the encouragement of community, and the fellowship of our churches, we faced epidemic loneliness, our suffering compounded by our isolation.

When we have nowhere left to turn, however, we discover an awareness of God's presence in our midst. He has been there all along, but in the hectic pace of our busy, distracted lives we often overlooked him. Sequestered and quarantined by the pandemic, we now have fewer distractions and obstacles impeding our need. We have never been in control of our lives, but it took recent events to shatter our illusion that we are self-sufficient.

In the midst of such vulnerability, desperation, and unvarnished need we realize that God has a gift for us behind closed doors. Don't believe me? You will recall that after His resurrection, Jesus appeared to His disciples not before an open door but behind a closed door: "That evening, the disciples gathered together. And because they were afraid of reprisals from the Jewish leaders, they had locked the doors to the place where they met. But suddenly Jesus appeared among them and said, 'Peace to you!'" (John 20:19, TPT).

We quarantined ourselves in order to survive.

But God set us apart so we can thrive!

THE BIG REVEAL

As difficult as it may be for you to accept, consider that sometimes closed doors have much more value than open ones. Why? Because a closed door precedes an open door. The two go together like day and night, light and dark. Until you wait behind a closed door, you cannot experience its outward movement toward expansion.

A closed door is about preparation.

An open door is about revelation.

A closed door is about equipping.

An open door is about elevation.

A closed door is God operating in you.

An open door is you operating through Christ in the world around you.

When the door closes, God changes you.

When the door opens, you change the world!

Therefore, do not mistake the temporary for the permanent. Do not curse the momentary process necessary for the eternal harvest. Before the disciples changed the world, they met with Jesus behind a closed door. After suffering the agonizing grief of losing their Master, after witnessing the horror of His torturous death on a cross like a common criminal, and after enduring the scandalous rumors that now His tomb was empty, the disciples needed to know what was true.

They needed to get back to basics and start a new chapter of the ministry begun when Jesus called them to be fishers of men. They had to embrace their God-given purpose and prepare for the infusion of the Holy Spirit to empower their lives. They needed a reboot in order to recharge their spiritual batteries and restart the process of living. They required a revelation that could only happen behind closed doors.

During these devastating and discouraging times of upheaval and downcast hearts, we must do the same. We must be patient and wait for the big reveal God has for us. So instead of resisting the confinement you have experienced, see its value as a gift. When His followers experienced the fullness of Christ's presence in their midst, they knew firsthand that the basis of their faith was true. The disciples not only heard Jesus, not only saw Jesus, but one of them actually *touched* Jesus in order to dispel his doubts.

> Now Thomas (also known as Didymus), one of the Twelve, was not with the disciples when Jesus came. So the other disciples told him, "We have seen the Lord!"
> But he said to them, "Unless I see the nail marks in his hands and put my finger where the nails were, and put my hand into his side, I will not believe."

A week later his disciples were in the house again, and Thomas was with them. Though the doors were locked, Jesus came and stood among them and said, "Peace be with you!" Then he said to Thomas, "Put your finger here; see my hands. Reach out your hand and put it into my side. Stop doubting and believe."

Thomas said to him, "My Lord and my God!"

Then Jesus told him, "Because you have seen me, you have believed; blessed are those who have not seen and yet have believed."

—JOHN 20:24–29

Thomas confessed that he wouldn't believe until he placed his finger in the wounds where Jesus' hands had been pierced by the spikes that were driven through to secure His outstretched body to crossbeams of wood. As much as Thomas may have wanted to believe that all Jesus had said during their time together was true, the disciple needed proof. He wanted evidence. He had to see for himself in order to restore his confidence and reboot his faith.

Notice that Jesus did not chastise or condemn Thomas' doubts. Instead, He provided the proof His follower needed in order to strengthen Thomas' faith. You see, God understands how hard it is for us to go through the unexpected, unimaginable ordeal of the coronavirus pandemic. He knows the fears and doubts plaguing our minds and hearts as we ruminate on our unpaid bills and lost employment. The Lord hears your prayers to keep your body healthy and free of the dangerous attacks of this unprecedented virus. Our heavenly Father knows we are afraid, and like the loving parent we would want to be with our own children, He doesn't threaten or shame us for expressing our fears and doubts.

Instead, our God does what is necessary to reassure us. To restore us. To strengthen us. He is always willing to meet us where we are. Simply stated, sometimes God will close the door in order to reveal something you otherwise would not see. Something personal and private. Something intimate.

- A closed door with Jesus permits revelation.
- A closed door with Jesus restores intimacy.
- A closed door with Jesus enables an encounter like never before.

Therefore, if you resent being locked away from the way things used to be, if you struggle to understand why you had to endure time in quarantine, then it's time to reframe your perceptions. It's time to resee your experiences of late through eternal eyes. It's time to focus on the invisible, not merely the tangible. It's time to believe even when you can't see everything you might wish to see. If you feel like the door has closed in front of you, then look again.

When you are living in the Spirit, a closed door only means that you are about to touch Jesus and experience His grace in an unprecedented manner. Your closed-door season provides the foundation for your open-door season. The doors you want God to open for you can only be revealed if you're willing to wait on His timing.

God is a God of making openings where there are none. He can open a door, and He can close a door. His Word explains, "This is the message from the one who is holy and true, the one who has the key of David. What he opens, no one can close; and what he closes, no one can open" (Rev. 3:7, NLT).

The door was locked, but Jesus passed through it. Just as He had faced death and defeated it, He overcame the seemingly permanent lock it held over humankind. Sealed in a cave with a boulder blocking the entrance, Jesus' lifeless body was laid to rest—temporarily, at least, because on the third day, the stone was rolled away. On the third day, His tomb was empty. On the third day, Jesus rose again!

In other words, Jesus might as well have told His disciples, "Hey, friends, there was a stone in front of the tomb, and yet I came out. If I can go through a stone, I can go through a door!" Our Savior had to sacrifice Himself on the cross in order to save us from our sins. He had to be placed inside the tomb, behind a closed door, before He could roll away the stone and emerge victorious over death.

Locked doors cannot stop someone with resurrection power!

BATTLE SCARS

When our children were small, they would run to us with the smallest scrape or the tiniest cut. "Look at my owie!" they would cry, wanting us to kiss it and make them feel better. Often we were not even able to see the imaginary wound or minor scratch affording them the opportunity to get loving attention from Mom and Dad. As they grew older, they learned that not every bump or boo-boo required a Band-Aid and the accompanying parental comfort. Finally, as adults, they realize that certain scars linger as reminders of the wounds that have been overcome.

When Jesus revealed His wounds to His disciples, He displayed the ultimate battle scars. He showed them His wounds and His side where the soldier's sword had pierced His body. This was not bravado, outrage, or a child's ploy for attention, though. Jesus was not showcasing His wounds as if to say, "Can you believe what they did to Me?" or "Have pity on Me!" or even "I can't believe I went through this." In today's social media parlance, some of us might start #nomorecrosses! But that's not what Jesus did.

On the contrary, He showed His wounds and His pierced side to confirm His identity as the Son of God. Jesus was not showing what others did to Him; Jesus was showing what He did for them—and for us! He was not simply revealing His wounds and stripes. More importantly, Christ was showing the disciples their forgiveness and healing, fulfilling the prophecy given by Isaiah: "But he was pierced because of our rebellion, crushed because of our iniquities; punishment for our peace was on him, and we are healed by his wounds" (Isa. 53:5, CSB).

When you see the wounds of Jesus, you see your forgiveness.

When you glimpse the stripes of Christ, you witness the source of your healing.

Only up close and personal, behind a closed door, could Jesus allow those closest to Him to see the price He paid for them to have eternal life. We're told "He himself carried our sins in his body on the cross so that we would be dead to sin and live for righteousness. Our instant healing flowed from his wounding" (1 Pet. 2:24, TPT).

You are forgiven to forgive.

You are healed to heal!

Behind closed doors you see the wounds that forgave you and the stripes that healed you! No matter what Jesus suffered, He paid the price and defeated death for all of us! The enemy tried to destroy Him, kill Him, and bury Him, but there He was! His message to His disciples then is the same for us today: "If I can survive, then you can thrive!"

Don't let the wounds and trauma of the recent past seal you in a tomb. Don't let the piercings drain the life and energy out of your spirit. Don't let all you've lost leave you dead to all that God has for you ahead. Instead of complaining about what the virus took from you, start proclaiming all that God has done for you. Whatever the price of enduring the fears, doubts, worries, anxieties, pains, injuries, and devastation of late, do not overlook the gift of grace you have received and the presence of God's Spirit dwelling in you.

Jesus paid the price so you can show something else.

Christ showed His wounds so we can show our healing.

Christ showed His piercing so we can show our peace.

When you complain and wallow in your wishful thinking, you're living in the past. You're using regret as a way to lock yourself in so that there's no way out. Jesus broke that lock, though, and met with you behind that door. He showed you His wounds so that you can know you are healed and will not only survive all the recent circumstances but will thrive in the power of the Holy Spirit!

So stop subsidizing the devil's marketing budget. Focus on what the Lord has done. Praise Him for the ways He has sustained you and brought you through all the turmoil, calamity, and chaos. Rejoice in the gifts of His Spirit.

Look what the Lord has done!

SPIRITUAL BREATHING

When you're faced with something impossible to handle, it can cause you to have a panic attack. Your body begins reacting as if you are in the midst of battle trauma. You feel paralyzed with fear or energized to fight. In those moments you have to hit pause and remember to breathe. When you feel like you're about to lose your mind, you must catch your breath.

When you feel trapped in quarantine without a way out, remember that God meets you there. When you assume you're ill-equipped to face the giant looming before you, remember that you have been given all you need. Everything you have endured up until this point has prepared you to survive in order to thrive.

Faced with an overwhelming opponent, David did not panic

but instead realized how his past had fortified him to overcome in the present. While his brothers groused, other soldiers ran, and the kind chided him for his naïve confidence,
David recalled how God had empowered him to defeat prior
dangers. He told King Saul:

> Your servant has been keeping his father's sheep. When
> a lion or a bear came and carried off a sheep from the
> flock, I went after it, struck it and rescued the sheep from
> its mouth. When it turned on me, I seized it by its hair,
> struck it and killed it. Your servant has killed both the
> lion and the bear; this uncircumcised Philistine will be
> like one of them, because he has defied the armies of the
> living God. The LORD who rescued me from the paw of
> the lion and the paw of the bear will rescue me from the
> hand of this Philistine.
>
> —1 SAMUEL 17:34–37

How has God equipped you to survive the present threat of
unfavorable circumstances? How has He sustained you with
the experience, skill, and tenacity to vanquish the virus and all
the collateral damage it wants to do? I suspect there are more
ways than you might see at first. And regardless of how many
lions and bears come to mind, you have what you need right
now if you will only take a deep breath.

You see, that's what Jesus did with His disciples in that Upper
Room that night: "Then, taking a deep breath, he blew on them
and said, 'Receive the Holy Spirit'" (John 20:22, TPT). After His
resurrection and before His followers changed the world, Jesus
took a deep breath. He breathed new life into their weary souls.

To a great degree we as humanity are collectively taking a
deep breath. COVID-19 prompted all of us to take a deep breath.
We had to stop running and doing and shelter in the presence
of the Almighty. After the resurrection, Jesus appeared behind

closed doors to His disciples, who were quarantined with fear, and breathed fresh air into them.

We shouldn't be surprised, really, because God first created us by breathing life into us: "Then the LORD God formed the man from the dust of the ground. He breathed the breath of life into the man's nostrils, and the man became a living person" (Gen. 2:7, NLT). The Hebrew word for *breath* here is *ruach*, which literally means putting air in motion, a puff of life, inhaling and exhaling with sustaining power.[2] We see this meaning echoed in the passage from John when Jesus breathes the Holy Spirit into His disciples. The Greek word used there, *pneuma*, means both breath and spirit.[3]

So when we feel stuck in solitude, languishing in lockdown, or quelled in quarantine, we must ask for a breath of spiritual air, a new instilling of God's Spirit in us. Like others before us we proclaim, "For the Spirit of God has made me, and the breath of the Almighty gives me life" (Job 33:4, NLT). When a baby is born, he has to breathe in order to activate his lungs. When we are born again, we receive God's Spirit to activate our new life as forgiven children of heaven and coheirs with Christ. New beginnings, open doors, and fresh starts always begin with a breath of life from God!

The Lord never changes, and His spiritual air supply is unlimited. During the COVID-19 crisis, so many people died because they could not breathe properly with the virus attacking their lungs and respiratory system. Ventilators became scarce necessities in the battle for those fighting the virus. But there is never any danger of running out of the fresh air of God's Spirit! He continues to breathe new life into us so that we can recover our physical, mental, emotional, and spiritual health.

God never changes! He is the same yesterday, today, and forever more. God continues to breathe into you right now even as you read these words. I believe by faith through Christ that the same God that breathed in Genesis and breathed in John is right now breathing into your family, breathing into your faith, breathing into your future, breathing into your finances, breathing into your health, breathing into your mind, breathing into your household, breathing into your children and your children's children.

Inhale the fresh, life-giving air of God's breath!

ONE AND ONLY ONE

Coming out of quarantine, as you recover from all you've experienced lately, you must realize that your destiny is not based on what's in front of you. Your destiny is based on the One who is inside of you! When Jesus appeared behind those closed doors, the spirit He released upon His disciples was His own Spirit of Holiness. In other words, it wasn't just any spirit—it was *the* Spirit!

This truth is important to remember because we see a number of other spirits mentioned in Scripture:

The spirit of divination (Acts 16:16–18)

The spirit of jealousy (Gal. 5:19–21)

The spirit of deception/lying (Rev. 12:10)

The spirit of perversion (2 Pet. 2:14)

The spirit of heaviness (Isa. 61:3)

The spirit of fear (2 Tim. 1:7)

The spirit of death (Luke 10:19)

The spirit of antichrist (1 John 2:18–19)

Amidst this variety of spirits I daresay there is one and *only* one that is the Holy Spirit of the living God!

Who is this Holy Spirit? The same Holy Spirit of Genesis that hovered upon the face of the deep, brought things to life, and created order out of disorder: "In the beginning God created the heavens and the earth. Now the earth was formless and empty, darkness was over the surface of the deep, and the Spirit of God was hovering" (Gen. 1:1–2). This is the same Spirit that filled Joshua, enabling him to survive the desert, cross over the Jordan, shout down the walls of Jericho, and step into the Promised Land (Num. 27:18).

This is the same Spirit that came upon a shepherd boy, enabling him to defeat the giant called Goliath, to conquer the city of Jerusalem and bring back the ark of the covenant. From the moment David was identified by God's prophet as the Lord's choice for king, the Spirit filled him: "Then Samuel took the horn of oil and anointed him in the midst of his brothers. And the Spirit of the LORD rushed upon David from that day forward" (1 Sam. 16:13, ESV).

If you want to experience this same kind of power, then breathe in. If you want order instead of chaos and you want life instead of being lifeless; if you desire to come out of your desert, cross over the Jordan, shout down the obstacles in front of you and step into your promised land; if you want to bring down the giants, possess your destiny, and bring back the glory, then understand this: the Holy Spirit is absolutely essential!

You are not just a human being—you are a spiritual being. You do not only occupy space; you house divinity. "Do you not know that you are God's temple and that God's Spirit dwells in you?" (1 Cor. 3:16, ESV). You're not just another person; you are a temple of the Holy Spirit. And when you receive the breath of Jesus, when you receive the Holy Spirit, when His exhale becomes your inhale, He does not temporarily occupy your space—He permanently fills your life!

You are not holy based on what you do.

You are holy based on whom you house.

So when I say there's greatness inside of you, I'm not engaging in prophetic hyperbole. I am speaking biblical truth. When the Holy Spirit lives inside of you, then rest assured:

There's royalty inside of you.

There's creative genius inside of you.

There's awesomeness inside of you.

There is love inside of you.

There is joy inside of you.

There is peace inside of you.

There is patience inside of you.

There is meekness inside of you.

There is goodness inside of you.

There is gentleness inside of you.

There is temperance inside of you.

There is mercy inside of you.

There is faith inside of you.

There is beauty inside of you!

BREATH AND POWER

When Jesus' breath becomes your source of life, you begin to thrive. When His exhale becomes your inhale, when His breath becomes your oxygen, when His Spirit becomes your life force, you live empowered! With this breath of life comes power: "But you will receive power when the Holy Spirit comes" (Acts 1:8).

Simply stated, you cannot claim to have the Holy Spirit and be powerless. There is no such animal as a powerless child of God. There is no such thing as a powerless question. There is no such thing as a powerless Christ follower. There is no such thing as a powerless person filled with the Spirit of God. When you inhale God's exhale, when you open up your heart and receive God's Spirit, then you have power—unlimited, inexhaustible power to do what others say is impossible, what you know cannot be done on your own!

> You have power to move mountains.
>
> You have power to cast out darkness.
>
> You have power over fear.
>
> You have power over anxiety.
>
> You have power over depression.
>
> You have power over your past.
>
> You have power over the old you.

You have the power you need to do the work of God, live out the Word of God, walk in the way of God, listen to the whisper of God, look through the windows of God, and change the world for God!

PRIVATE BEFORE PUBLIC

As we move from surviving to thriving, we realize that we must do more than merely breathe in the power of God's Spirit. We must also release that holy breath into the lives of others. If all we do is breathe in, then we die. We must exhale even as we must inhale.

Sometimes you will encounter people who only want to breathe in without ever letting go of what they've taken in. They rely on the energy of others and literally seem to suck the air out of the room when you're with them. They inhale and spiritually hold their breath. No wonder, then, they're blue in the face!

When you're filled with God's Spirit, you begin to practice spiritual breathing. You inhale and exhale, trusting both are necessary for you to survive and then to thrive. With patience and wisdom we discover the following:

Breathing in is receiving. Breathing out is giving.

Breathing in is sowing. Breathing out is reaping.

Breathing in is binding. Breathing out is releasing.

Breathing in makes you a listener of the Word. Breathing out makes you a doer of the Word.

Breathing in makes you a consumer. Breathing out makes you a producer!

Behind closed doors, in the holy quarantine, Jesus Christ, after His resurrection, breathed in and breathed out. And when He exhaled, He blew upon His disciples the most essential element not just for us to survive but for us to thrive—His Holy Spirit! As we find ourselves quarantined, whether literally or figuratively, let us not forget what is most essential: an intimate relationship with God the Father, God the Son, and God the Holy Spirit.

Remember, it's what you do behind closed doors that will determine what you will see when the doors are open. Closed doors precede open doors. Closed doors represent the private; open doors represent the public. It's what you do in privacy that will determine what you will do in the public sphere. Your private life will determine your public life.

Jesus died publicly and then privately showed the disciples His wounds so they could demonstrate His power publicly. We're assured, "Then Jesus made a public spectacle of all the powers and principalities of darkness, stripping away from them every weapon and all their spiritual authority and power to accuse us. And by the power of the cross, Jesus led them around as prisoners in a procession of triumph. *He was not their prisoner; they were his!*" (Col. 2:15, TPT).

What we do behind closed doors will determine what we see with open doors.

It's time to get your behind-closed-doors life aligned with God so your open-door life can thrive. Frequently the problem is that people want to fight their giant in the open when they're not willing to fight the giant behind what is closed. You must win your private battles before you try to fight your public giants. You must worship and be empowered alone with God before you attempt to do it in front of others. Because once you overcome inside, you can overcome outside!

When you submit to the Lamb in private, then you can crush the serpent in public. You must pass through the narrow way in your heart before you can walk the red carpet in the world. You must put God first before you take your first step through an open door. You encounter God before you encounter the world. God changes you before you change the world!

As followers of Jesus we are called to be set apart, sanctified, and transformed into the likeness of our Savior. While we may feel claustrophobic at first, when we retreat into stillness and intimacy with God, we discover the liberation and power that comes from His Spirit. We are never isolated from God, nor can we be quarantined and cut off from His presence.

We are His children created in His image to thrive!

ALIVE TO THRIVE

Once again, use the following questions to help you reflect on this chapter's message and apply it to your own life. While it's not required, I encourage you to write down your responses so you can refer back to them later. After you've spent a few moments thinking about your answers to these questions, go to the Lord in prayer and share with Him the giants looming in your heart. As before, a short prayer is included to help you get started, but make it your own as you talk to your Father.

1. How has experiencing the recent pandemic and accompanying challenges affected your relationship with God? When were you struggling the most and feeling at your lowest? How did God meet you there?

2. When have you experienced intimacy and closeness with God during recent times of isolation and aloneness? What did the Lord reveal to you about Himself during this time? What did He show you about your future?

3. What does spiritual breathing look like in your life right now? How have you experienced a fresh breath of God's Spirit lately? How has this produced new life as you breathe out holy power to others?

Dear Lord, I continue to battle many of the same fears, anxieties, and worries even when I know You have given me all I need not only to survive but to thrive. Strengthen my faith, Jesus, even as You assured Your disciples in the Upper Room after Your resurrection. Empower me to do all that You have called me to do. Help me catch my breath so that I can begin this new season of life and walk through the door You are opening before me. Amen.

Chapter 3

HEALED BY FAITH—UNMASK GOD'S POWER

No matter what we encounter,
we must rely on God's power, not our own, for healing.

Healing occurs when we reach out and touch Jesus!

URING THE CORONAVIRUS pandemic, masks became symbols of life or death. Once used only by health-care professionals in dire situations or by first responders going into hazardous scenes with smoke, gas, or toxic chemicals, masks provide buffers to filter out harmful germs and polluted air. As COVID-19 transmission was scrutinized, doctors and scientists realized the essential benefits of wearing masks in almost all situations involving exposure or close proximity to others. Masks prevented particles of saliva and other microscopic, airborne viral agents from contact with our faces and entryway into our mouths and nostrils.

Suddenly masks became yet another scarce resource for those on the front line of treating patients and those with compromised immune systems prone to the virus. Along with hand sanitizer and antibacterial soap for conscientious cleansing, masks were essential items for survival. To go without a mask meant increasing the risk of contracting an invisible enemy with the power to ravage your body and steal your life.

As the sight of crowds, handshakes, hugs, and waiting lines

elbow-to-elbow faded from memory, the image of individuals wearing masks took its place. While many masks were disposable and made of paper, the shortage necessitated that many doctors and nurses wore them until they were literally threadbare. Countless tailors, designers, seamstresses, and crafters began making masks to ensure their availability to everyone in need. Suddenly fabric masks in bold colors, prints, and plaids showed up. People recycled old garments and materials on hand to create barriers to protect their mouths and noses.

Once businesses and stores began to reopen, masks provided a kind of shield as people returned to familiar locations forever changed. Slowly and gradually many people abandoned masks with cautious optimism. While they no longer relied on them to shield them from the coronavirus, people continued to mask their hopes for a return to normal. We all knew nothing would ever quite be the same. Even with the imminent development of a vaccine and new insight into prevention, even for those of us who were blessed with ongoing health and safety, healing would still be required—for minds, hearts, and spirits.

Even as great strides have been made, we continue to need the kind of supernatural healing that can only come from God. Healing to restore grieving families and those battling depression. Healing for the financial blows dealt by employment and a faltering economy. Healing for anxious millennials and fearful elders, for distraught leaders and struggling survivors. Healing to move on from a season whose scars will linger for years to come.

WILLING AND ABLE

Long before the coronavirus sent us urgently searching for vaccines and treatments, for ventilators and masks, people often told me that they were unable to slay the giants in their lives because of their limitations, their losses, their wounds. They felt inhibited, impaired, and impeded from being the kind of conqueror God calls each of us to be. While the kind of wounding may vary with each individual, the lingering effects are often similar: fear, doubt, anxiety, depression, worry, anger, and uncertainty.

With the advent of the pandemic, new fears trigger old traumatic reactions. We don't know if we will remain healthy, if our loved ones will recover, if we will have enough money, if we can continue to live in our present homes. Our bodies fight exhaustion as depression and anxiety take their toll. We feel consumed by the ever-churning sensationalism of the 24/7 news cycle, afraid to check out for long but equally terrified to keep checking.

No one escaped the pain, suffering, discomfort, and inconvenience caused by COVID-19. Regardless of our age, where we lived, our level of education and income, our race and cultural ethnicity, whether Christian or atheist, no human being escaped feeling the impact of the pandemic.

Similarly, all of us have wounds, including followers of Jesus. But the crucial difference for believers is that our wounds lead us to rely on God's power and not our own. We discover that our injuries, wounds, and scars become prisms facilitating and magnifying what the Lord can do through our lives. They can even become beacons showing others the majesty and magnificence of supernatural healing and spiritual wholeness. When we experience what we cannot do for ourselves—what no human being can do for us—then everyone around us sees God at work in our lives. Our humility keeps us tethered to God's healing power in us and through us!

There are laws that govern healing, however. God makes it clear that we have to be willing for Him to work in our lives. We have to remove the masks we hide behind as well as the filters we use to distance ourselves from Him. We have to face the spiritual obstacles that are within our power to remove in order for God's Spirit to work freely in our lives and bring about healing. If our relationship with God is not in order, then we get in the way of our own healing. We must be willing to be healed and able to align our hearts and lives with the Holy Spirit.

Keep in mind, too, that the devil wants you sick, broken, and wounded. He wants to take you out and leave you limping instead of walking by faith and running in the power of your Redeemer. This is the power Jesus won for us through His death on the cross and resurrection as He defeated sin and death once and for all: "Jesus of Nazareth was anointed by God with the Holy Spirit and with great power. He did wonderful things for others and divinely healed all who were under the tyranny of the devil, for God had anointed him" (Acts 10:38, TPT).

God's Word outlines three deterrents to our healing: unforgiveness, unbelief, and unrepentance. Forgiveness is inherent to how we relate to God and to others. In the Lord's Prayer, Jesus instructed us to pray, "Forgive us our sins, as we have forgiven those who sin against us" (Matt. 6:12, NLT). Because God has shown such great mercy and amazing grace to us in the midst of our sinfulness, we are to share it with those around us. When we refuse to forgive others, we are basically elevating our standards above and beyond the grace and mercy of our perfect Holy God! When we refuse to forgive *ourselves*, we are doing the same thing and allowing our pride, guilt, shame, and fear to paralyze us.

Similarly, our unbelief applies to how we live our lives as much as to what we believe. In other words, do we walk what we talk? It's not only our own doubts that get in the way of God's healing presence and power in our lives, but it's also the doubts of others. The unbelief of those around you can become as contagious as the COVID-19 virus and infect your thinking with doubts, worries, and anxieties. Your relationships reflect what you believe and reveal how you practice your beliefs.

When you harbor sin in your life and refuse to surrender it, you create an infection that blocks the divine flow of God's healing power: unrepentance. Instead of admitting your sin and turning back to God and obediently following His ways, you follow your own path. Even after you have been saved by the blood of Christ, if you refuse to follow Him and obey God, then your rebellion becomes a barrier to all that His Spirit wants to do in your life. You can't be healed unless you follow the Holy!

The remedy to these three impediments is revealed in Scripture as well:

> Are any of you sick? You should call for the elders of the church to come and pray over you, anointing you with oil in the name of the Lord. Such a prayer offered in faith will heal the sick, and the Lord will make you well. And if you have committed any sins, you will be forgiven.
>
> Confess your sins to each other and pray for each other so that you may be healed. The earnest prayer of a righteous person has great power and produces wonderful results.
>
> —JAMES 5:14–16, NLT

Notice the factors mentioned here that open the door to healing: prayer and anointing, repentance and confession. Notice, too, the importance of relationships within the community of believers. If you're sick and in need of healing, then ask the elders of your church to pray over you and anoint you with oil. Confess your sins to one another and lift up your brothers and sisters in prayer, calling upon the name of the Lord for His healing power. When you turn to God, forgive others as well as yourself, and believe in the power of His Spirit, you know that you will be healed!

LOST AND FOUND

Easier said than done, right? I know having this kind of faith in the power of God to heal you is no small thing. When we suffer injury, betrayal, pain, and emotional anguish in life, we're tempted to see ourselves as victims rather than victors in Christ Jesus. Our suffering feels so powerful and immediate that we struggle to see how we can go on. But that's just it—we *can't* go on unless we rely on God's power! We may never make sense of our life's losses and sad events, but we don't have to understand them when we place our faith in the Lord.

This is the powerful lesson we see illustrated by the dual healings of a desperate woman who had been suffering for a dozen years and a little girl restored to life. The fact that these two intersect is no coincidence, of course, as we see Jesus delayed by one encounter before He can get to the other:

> After Jesus returned from across the lake, a huge crowd of people quickly gathered around him on the shoreline. Just then, a man saw that it was Jesus, so he pushed through the crowd and threw himself down at his feet. His name was Jairus, a Jewish official who was in charge of the synagogue. He pleaded with Jesus, saying over and over, "Please come with me! My little daughter is at the point of death, and she's only twelve years old! Come and lay your hands on her and heal her and she will live!"
>
> Jesus went with him, and the huge crowd followed, pressing in on him from all sides.
>
> Now, in the crowd that day was a woman who had suffered horribly from continual bleeding for twelve years. She had endured a great deal under the care of various doctors, yet in spite of spending all she had on their treatments, she was not getting better, but worse. When she heard about Jesus' healing power, she pushed through the crowd and came up from behind him and touched

his prayer shawl. For she kept saying to herself, "If only I could touch his clothes, I know I will be healed." As soon as her hand touched him, her bleeding immediately stopped! She knew it, for she could feel her body instantly being healed of her disease!

—MARK 5:21–29, TPT

In order to live a healed life, this woman had to break through both her internal angst and the external crowd. Inside she was consumed by her past (suffering for twelve years), her present (she was broke), and her future (her condition was getting worse). Outside, countless people stood in between her need and her hope, Christ. This woman did not have the resources, funding, or hope in the medical profession of her day. She had no money, no health care, no insurance, no Obamacare!

Inside, however, this woman had the only necessary resource for her healing: *faith*! Instead of focusing on all that she lacked, she channeled all her strength and energy into exercising the mustard seed of faith she had in Jesus. She believed she didn't even need to introduce herself, explain her situation, and beg for healing. She had faith that if she could just graze the hem of His robe with her fingertips, she would be healed!

What about you? What do you have?

It's time to stop focusing on all that you lack, on all that you wish you had, and instead give God praise for what you do have! Stop whining about what's missing and start shouting about what you've found! Nothing you've lost compares to finding Jesus!

You have a faith that moves mountains.

You have a shout that brings down walls.

You have joy that cannot be explained.

You have a peace that passes all understanding.

You have a grace that is sufficient.

You have an anointing that destroys the yoke.

You have a gift that cannot be revoked.

You have a destiny that cannot be stopped.

You have mercies that are new every morning.

You have the strength of the Father, the grace of the Son, and the anointing of the Holy Spirit! When you serve God with what you have, He will take care of what you need. Faith requires you to trust God even when you do not understand Him, moving forward in obedience and gratitude when life makes no sense. Faith unmasks your fears and unleashes the power of God's Spirit to bring healing and restoration.

Faith requires you to push through in order to experience your breakthrough!

"WHEN" NOT "IF"

This woman not only had to overcome her physical suffering, emotional fears, and spiritual doubts, but she also had to push through the crowd to reach her miracle. Jesus was surrounded by other people even as He purposefully moved through the throngs toward His destination, which we know was Jairus' house. Men, women, and children swarmed around Him as Jairus tried to lead the only hope he had for his daughter to her bedside. But the tenacious faith of this woman in need would not allow her to be deterred by all that surrounded Jesus!

We often face the same challenge in order to experience our healing. Because once again, Jesus is often surrounded— by dogma and legalism. Surrounded by bureaucracies and constructs of culture and personal philosophies that impede us from touching the living power and presence of Christ. Exercising the same faith-fueled determination as this precious woman, you must break through the ideas, rituals, dogmas, legalism, bureaucracy, religiosity, and erroneous interpretations that surround the person, the life, the ministry, the power, and the presence of Jesus Christ. Sometimes we surround God with all this stuff of our own making that is simply unnecessary and irrelevant. We get in our own way and make it hard for the broken to reach Him and receive the healing He offers!

This woman broke through all that stood between her and her Healer—the stigma of her disease, the assaults on her reputation, the contempt of others, the skepticism of her doctors, her own fears and suffering. She went through in order to get to!

You see, all of us must understand that we have to go through to get to. The psalmist said, "Even when I walk through the darkest valley, I will not be afraid, for you are close beside me. Your rod and your staff protect and comfort me" (Ps. 23:4, NLT). Notice he said *"when* I walk" and not *"if* I walk through the darkest valley." He knew that everyone goes through times like the one we've experiencing because of the COVID-19 virus. Whether circumstances seem distinctly personal or compounded on a global scale, we all need the healing power and presence of God in our midst.

The prophet Isaiah also knew that it's a matter of "when" and not "if." He wrote, "When you go through deep waters, I will be with you. When you go through rivers of difficulty, you will not drown. When you walk through the fire of oppression, you will not be burned up; the flames will not consume you" (Isa. 43:2, NLT).

I suspect you have already pushed through in order to break through at least one big challenge in your life, at least one big riptide beneath floodwaters, at least one big firestorm scorching everything you care about. Maybe you've been through a couple or several or so many that you feel like Job! Regardless of the quantity, however, let me ask you: *Why are you still here?* Why are you still alive and reading the words on this page? Why are you daring to tell all the trolls, naysayers, critics, and enemies, "Oh yeah? *Just watch me*"?

It's not because of your personality, good looks, intellectual acumen, spiritual fortitude, or economic wherewithal. It's because the purpose of God is greater than your brokenness!

It's not because you perfectly held on to God.

It's because God perfectly held on to you.

BROKEN FOR A BREAKTHROUGH

This woman was broken, and yet she touched God. Her faith-filled gesture reminds us that not only can God reach the broken, but the broken can reach out to Him! This broken woman pushed through the crowd, moved beyond everyone and everything surrounding Jesus, and reached out her hand to touch Him. She was broken and yet broke through!

This dear lady reminds us that you don't have to be perfect to receive God's love and to experience His healing power. God uses imperfect people to advance His perfect agenda. He uses broken people that dare touch Him to heal a broken world! Christianity is less about promoting the perfect and more about blessing the broken.

We're assured that God never rejects the broken (Ps. 51:17). Broken people understand that you're not holy because of what you do but because of what God has done for you. The Lord's purposes are always greater than our brokenness. He has always delighted in creating great things from our broken pieces. We know that in Christ, nothing—absolutely *nothing*—is beyond repair.

God can fix everything!

If it's broken, God can mend it.

If it's empty, God can fill it.

If it failed, God can restore it.

If it sinned, God can forgive it.

If it's wrong, God can make it right.

If it's crooked, God can make it straight.

If it fell, God can pick it up.

And if it died, God can resurrect it!

Nothing is beyond God—no matter what, He can do it!

I have experienced this firsthand in so many ways, time and time again. When I started the National Hispanic Christian Leadership Conference (NHCLC), many people did not take me or our organization seriously. They viewed what we were doing as a pleasant way for Hispanic pastors to connect and share cultural commonalities. They couldn't see that we were about serving all people in ways that unite the body of Christ, spread the good news of the gospel, and bring the power of God's Spirit to everyone around the world.

When I first started making inroads in Washington, DC, as a voice for Christian leaders and Hispanic people of faith, I received many polite handshakes and benign smiles. No one wanted to dismiss me because it would be considered politically incorrect, but no one knew what to do with me either! Slowly a few people began to listen to what I had to say, to introduce me to other leaders, and then to solicit my viewpoint on various topics and issues.

Even as I found myself meeting with members of Congress, I never dreamed that I would one day be shaking the hand of the president of the United States, let alone praying at the inauguration of yet another president before almost millions of people worldwide! But I kept reaching, stretching, extending myself as I stepped out in faith and followed the Spirit's guidance along the way. Just like the woman touching the hem of the Savior's garment, I'm living proof that nothing is impossible with God!

And so are you! Let nothing deter you from reaching out to experience the power of Jesus. Will you dare to push through everything around Him and feel His presence?

JUST ONE TOUCH

This woman knew that it only takes one touch to access the healing power of the Messiah. Her faith led her to push through to her breakthrough, but as we see here, she also received something else from Jesus that day:

> Jesus knew at once that someone had touched him, for he felt the power that always surged around him had passed through him for someone to be healed. He turned and spoke to the crowd, saying, "Who touched my clothes?"
>
> His disciples answered, "What do you mean, who touched you? Look at this huge crowd—they're all pressing up against you." But Jesus' eyes swept across the crowd, looking for the one who had touched him for healing.
>
> When the woman who experienced this miracle realized what had happened to her, she came before him, trembling with fear, and threw herself down at his feet, saying, "I was the one who touched you." And she told him her story of what had just happened.

> Then Jesus said to her, "Daughter, because you dared to
> believe, your faith has healed you. Go with peace in your
> heart, and be free from your suffering!"
> —MARK 5:30–34, TPT

I love the fact that this woman thought she could sneak up on Jesus, get the healing power she needed, and never bother Him in the process. Being God's Son, of course, He knew right away that His power had been accessed. And the disciples' response cracks me up! They apparently thought Jesus was being facetious, basically responding, "Of course someone touched You! Look at all the people elbowing us in this crowd." But Jesus knew it was more than a casual brush against His arm or an accidental nudge.

Instead of running in fear, the recipient of His healing gift realized that He knew and fell on her feet before Him. If her Healer had the power to cure her, then He certainly had the power to know she had been healed. Jesus allowed her to tell her story, and then He blessed her! While this response might be the opposite of what we expect if He were anyone other than Christ, the Savior blessed her. It's almost as if He celebrated the audacity of her faith. "Daughter, because you dared to believe, your faith has healed you," Jesus told her. "Go with peace in your heart, and be free from your suffering!" (Mark 5:34, TPT).

This woman followed Jesus, she touched Him, and she received healing. Jesus wasn't looking at her but was on His way to heal a little girl, the next generation, when He sensed that someone had tapped into His power and been healed. He rewarded this woman's courage: she understood that if she entered into His presence, divine power would be released.

It's time for you to touch Him!

Stop waiting for God to touch you—it's time to get up and touch Him!

You are no longer waiting for a miracle, because there's a miracle waiting for you.

Immediate changes took place upon her touch. She was healed! Power came out of Jesus, so He turned around to see the cause. The woman humbled herself and spoke truth. She experienced the fullness of joy that comes from being in His presence (Ps. 16:1).

When the power of God heals us, the experience provokes a turnaround in our lives that enables us to have more than a testimony. It empowers us to speak truth. With just one touch, silence is no longer an option! Just as so many doctors tried to treat this woman's condition, it took the Great Physician to heal her fully and completely.

We can look to others for their opinions and diagnoses; we can try other sources of power for divine healing; we can even have faith—but if our faith is not founded on the living God and the power of His Spirit through the work of His Son, Jesus Christ, then it is futile. Jesus made it clear for us: "I am the way and the truth and the life. No one comes to the Father except through me" (John 14:6).

God wants to turn some things around in your life, but He's waiting on you to touch Him.

He wants to heal you, but you must stop looking elsewhere.

Jesus has the power and wants to heal you and bless you.

Will you reach out your hand in faith?

Can you feel the hem of His garment?

WAKE-UP CALL

After healing this woman and blessing her faith, Jesus proceeded to His destination and the need awaiting Him there, even though it appeared to be too late.

And before he had finished speaking, people arrived from Jairus' house and pushed through the crowd to give Jairus the news: "There's no need to trouble the master any longer—your daughter has died." But Jesus refused to listen to what they were told and said to the Jewish official, "Don't yield to fear. All you need to do is to keep on believing." So they left for his home, but Jesus didn't allow anyone to go with them except Peter and the two brothers, Jacob and John.

When they arrived at the home of the synagogue ruler, they encountered a noisy uproar among the people, for they were all weeping and wailing. Upon entering the home, Jesus said to them, "Why all this grief and weeping? Don't you know the girl is not dead but merely asleep?" Then everyone began to ridicule and make fun of him. But he threw them all outside.

Then he took the child's father and mother and his three disciples and went into the room where the girl was lying. He tenderly clasped the child's hand in his and said to her in Aramaic, "Talitha koum," which means, "Little girl, wake up from the sleep of death." Instantly the twelve-year-old girl sat up, stood to her feet, and started walking around the room! Everyone was overcome with astonishment in seeing this miracle!

—MARK 5:35–42, TPT

How many times have others told you to give up? How many people have insisted your dreams were dead, your hopes were dead, and your possibilities were dead? The number doesn't matter as long as you hear the Master's instruction: "Don't be afraid; just believe" (Mark 5:36). Even after Jesus arrived at Jairus' house, the mourners and critics scoffed at Him when He told them the girl was merely sleeping. They couldn't imagine such a possibility—they lacked faith! So Jesus sent them outside, away from the powerful miracle He then performed. The words Christ spoke, *Talitha koum*, reflect the power of His command even as it's addressed fondly to this "little girl." It's the most heavenly wake-up call that's ever existed!

No matter what you've lost or how much you're suffering, Jesus says it's time to wake up! Your doctors may tell you it's hopeless, scientists may be struggling for vaccines and cures, and your finances may be crippled worse than your body. Healing is not only possible—it's there waiting to wake you from the nightmare you've been living.

Many people have written off the church just as they dismiss those who follow Jesus. Many have prematurely written the obituary of Christianity. Many have declared that the next generation is spiritually dead on arrival. But none of it is true! The healing words of our Savior ring with truth for us today: "Don't be afraid. Just believe."

Believe in the Lord Jesus, and you will be saved.

Believe that no weapon formed against us shall prosper.

Believe that the latter glory will be greater than the former.

Believe that the gates of hell shall not, will not, cannot prevail against the church of Jesus Christ!

Believe, believe, believe!

—Talitha koum!

RISE AND SHINE

It takes radical, circumstance-shattering, life-altering, heaven-exciting, hell-upsetting faith to break through failure, rejection, shame, hurt, and brokenness. It takes faith in action day after day as you push through until your breakthrough. It requires tenacious faith that refuses to give up when everyone tells you that you're beyond hope and still declining. It requires willingness to reach out and touch God when it appears your dreams are dead.

To be healed is to be whole.

To be whole is to be complete.

To be complete is to live a life of shalom.

Nothing missing, nothing broken.

Wounded people wound people.

Broken people break people.

But healed people heal people.

God wants you healed!

God wants to use you to heal others in mind, body, and soul.

So child of God, rise up.

Rise up and walk like Enoch.

Rise up and believe like Abraham.

Rise up and dress like Joseph.

Rise up and stretch like Moses.

Rise up and shout like Joshua.

Rise up and dance like David.

Rise up and fight like Gideon.

Rise up and pray like Daniel.

Rise up and build like Nehemiah.

Rise up and shine like Jesus!

With just one touch, you can change the world!

ALIVE TO THRIVE

Reflect on your answers to the questions below and then spend some time before the Lord in prayer. Use this time to process what it means for you to experience healing in your life in the midst of your current circumstances. Open your heart and share all that you've suffered to get to this point. Reveal all the past wounds and uncover all your old scars. Invite God's Spirit to work in you, with you, through you. Reach out your hand in faith and feel the edge of heaven, knowing God is healing you.

1. What limitations and liabilities have kept you from going to battle with the giants in your path? When have you avoided a spiritual battle because you worried that your old wounds would get in the way?

2. When have you experienced the healing presence and power of God? How did you reach out and touch Him? How did He meet you in the midst of your need?

3. Have you given up on a dream and pronounced it dead too soon? Will you dare to believe Jesus can bring it back to life? What is the wake-up call you hear from God's Spirit right now? Where is He restoring life to what was once asleep?

Dear Lord, thank You for Your healing power at work in my life! I often feel afraid and lose sight of the confidence I have from You. I let old wounds and new worries prevent me from going to battle with the giants in my path. Give me courage to reach out and touch You, clinging to Your power, my Rock, my Redeemer, my radiant, radical Lord. Use my scars to heal others, Father. Open new territories of ministry through the battles I have already won through Your power. Let others see You shine through my struggles as I am made whole through Your supernatural presence in my life. Amen.

Chapter 4

HEART HEALTHY—SPREAD CONTAGIOUS JOY

*Your relationship with God is the source of
healthy living in every area of your life.*

*When you follow Jesus,
you know it is well with your soul!*

IN THE WAKE of the coronavirus, living a healthy life has taken on new meaning. We have learned the importance of handwashing, face-masking, and social distancing. Businesses have closed, some temporarily and some permanently, costing many of us our jobs and steady income. Kids have relied on online classrooms, while many parents have juggled working from home with childcare and, in many cases, eldercare. I don't need to remind you just how stressful this pandemic has been in its unprecedented assault on our bodies, our families, our communities, our careers, our finances, and our churches.

Through all of the hardships and requisite adjustments, though, God's definition of healthy living has not changed. It hasn't changed because His character, love, and goodness toward us His children never changes! His Word assures us, "Every good and perfect gift is from above, coming down from the Father of the heavenly lights, who does not change like shifting shadows" (Jas. 1:17). With the psalmist we can proclaim, "The LORD is my rock, my fortress and my deliverer; my God is my rock, in whom I take refuge, my shield and the horn of my salvation, my stronghold" (Ps. 18:2).

The enemy would have you believe that you can't live a healthy life in the wake of COVID-19. He wants you to feel like a victim of this virus, a prisoner of this pandemic, and a doubter of your destiny. But you and I know that nothing—not our enemy's assaults nor the viral germs' attacks on our immune systems—can remove us from the hand of God. Just as the Good Shepherd guards His flock and the loving Father shelters His children, our God has never abandoned us, and He's not about to start now!

Even amidst the devastating, ongoing impact of the global pandemic we must not lose sight of true health. As painful and agonizing as it has been to experience the virus in your body, to endure the loss of loved ones who succumbed to its assault, and to rebuild from the crater of economic recession and financial instability, the coronavirus will never rob you of a healthy spirit anchored to the power of our living God. The virus wants to mock you, shock you, and rock you, but it can never claim the ultimate victory because the battle belongs to the Lord!

You may have learned as I did that the coronavirus was named after the tiny points jutting out from the viral cell that make it appear like a crown, which is *corona* in Latin. There is nothing royal, regal, or reverential about this insidious killer, though. Like an invisible Goliath it has ravaged countless lives, claiming bodies and trying to infect our souls with a spirit of fear, of doubt, of despair. But no matter how powerful it has been or how much devastation it has wrought in your life, it will never win.

The viral crown can never replace the crown of thorns worn by the King of kings!

HOLY AND WHOLLY

Perhaps in the wake of the worldwide pandemic it's difficult to remember what healthy living means. In the collateral damage of all you've suffered, you may struggle to recall times in which your body enjoyed robust life and your spirit overflowed with the joy of the Lord. But do not allow the rose-colored glasses of nostalgia to distort your view. Even before the coronavirus, our definition of healthy living was not always the same as God's.

For years I defined it by the word that now seems as warped as a flat tire: *balance*. I pursued life-work balance; equilibrium in my relationships; balance at home, at church, at the office. I thought healthy living involved attending to my physical, emotional, relational, psychological, and spiritual needs in a way that kept them all level with one another. Like spokes on a wheel extending from a hub of well-being, these different areas needed to be in synchronicity in order for me to live a balanced, healthy life.

What I discovered, however, is that balance—at least the ideal I kept chasing—rarely exists. Life gets in the way. Ministry often consumes more time and energy than I allot in my schedule, spilling over into my time at home, my time to run and exercise my body, my time to fellowship with family and friends. Leadership roles require attention 24/7 in order to serve those in my care to the best of my ability. No matter how furiously I tried to devote equal portions of my time, energy, and attention to the priorities in my life, I never seemed to sustain it for more than a day, if that long.

So I stopped making balance a kind of idol. This realization does not mean that I stopped pursuing balance in the major areas of my life, only that I stopped feeling like a failure when one part consumed more of my time and attention than another. I quit trying to make balance more important than the priorities I was working so hard to juggle. God's Word tells us that "to everything there is a season" (Eccles. 3:1, NKJV), which means that following the Spirit's direction and omniscient wisdom is the basis for our priorities, not a human-determined ideal that we think we can control.

Healthy living is based on truth—the truth of God's Word; the truth about who you are, what you're doing, and whom you're doing it for. The truth about God's character, His power, and His love. The truth about Jesus' presence, His purpose, and His passion. The truth about the Spirit's residence in your heart, your life, and your body.

We see this kind of health reflected in John's prayer to Gaius: "Dear friend, I pray that you may enjoy good health and that all may go well with you, even as your soul is getting along well" (3 John 2). Rendered as "good health" in this translation, the Greek word *eudōomai* means "to be brought along to a smooth and prosperous journey" or "to be continually prospered [unto success] in every way."[1] The original word conveys a sense of alignment and motion working in harmony together. Basically John was praying that his friend's physical health would match his spiritual health.

God is similarly concerned for both our physical health and our spiritual well-being, along with all the facets these include—emotional, mental, psychological, and so on. If our Creator did not design us to experience this kind of wholeness, then why would John pray such a thing for his friend here, Gaius? This is the same kind of integrity, the same harmony of wholeness, displayed in Jesus' life. While the details of His maturation are not revealed, we're told that "Jesus grew in wisdom and stature, and in favor with God and man" (Luke 2:52).

In fact, this emphasis is reflected throughout the pages of Scripture. Created in the image of God and filled with His presence, we're instructed to honor our bodies as holy vessels: "Do you not know that your bodies are temples of the Holy

Spirit, who is in you, whom you have received from God? You are not your own; you were bought at a price. Therefore honor God with your bodies" (1 Cor. 6:19–20).

Healthy living is holy living and wholly living!

THE LION KING

When I consider healthy living, what it means to live with body and soul aligned to God's divine design, a vivid image comes to mind. I recall seeing a regal lion in an animal preserve during a recent ministry visit to South Africa. My hosts wanted me to experience the exquisite natural beauty of their homeland as well as to encounter some of its natural inhabitants. Consequently I was blessed to encounter so many native animals in the wild, for the most part living as they do in the untamed wilderness.

Although I have seen countless images of lions, including a few too many viewings of Disney's *The Lion King* when our kids were little, I was stunned by the majestic presence of the golden creature that I encountered there in an expansive animal preserve outside Johannesburg. With his wild, brassy mane framing his head like a sunburst, he stood still as a statue, poised and pensive, taking in the adoration of his small crowd of spectators. I was so moved that tears leaked from the corners of my eyes, which prompted me to recall a verse of Scripture about the mighty Lion of Judah, making my joy even more complete: "Stop weeping! Look, the Lion of the tribe of Judah, the heir to David's throne, has won the victory" (Rev. 5:5, NLT).

Later, as I reflected on the power in that special moment, I returned to that passage in Revelation and noticed the verse that followed the one I had recalled: "Then I saw a Lamb that looked as if it had been slaughtered, but it was now standing between the throne and the four living beings among the twenty-four elders" (Rev. 5:6, NLT). In John's transcendent vision he saw Christ as both Lion and Lamb, as strong and mighty as the former and as tender and pure as the latter.

When we put on Christ, when we claim our identity in Him, then we also put on Christ the Lamb of God and Christ the Lion of Judah! Just like our Savior we are defined by this paradoxical pairing of animals. We are both body and soul, lamb and lion. I suspect most of us find it easier to identify with the lamb than with the lion, perhaps because sheep tend to follow the flock, wander away from the fold, and remain defenseless against predators. We can often relate to feeling powerless and passive when our circumstances overwhelm us.

No matter how we feel, however, or how our circumstances may change, we know without a doubt the mighty and fierce power of the Lion of Judah is in us. You may feel like a lamb as you suffer in this life, but you roar like an eternal lion! You may appear weak and out of options to those around you, but that is when God's ferocious strength is perfected in you.

Now more than ever we must fully embrace what it means to be lions of light for God's kingdom. In a world full of hyenas, serpents, and wolves, it's time for holy lions to rise up. In a world wobbling to reclaim its balance after the coronavirus pandemic, we must be lions leading the way.

How do we do this?

It's really quite simple: Jesus is the Lion of Judah, and *Judah* means *praise*! Just as the mighty lion's roar can be heard throughout the jungle for almost five miles, we must raise our voices in praise of all God is doing so that everyone around us can hear the good news. Especially when we face challenges or experience suffering, how we respond and vocalize our faith carries enormous power. When others see healing in our lives, they glimpse God at work. When the world watches us slay our giants, it recognizes prophetic power.

In the natural world lions also use their roar to mark their territory. As far as their anthem of ownership can be heard, they are king within those audible boundaries. The enemies of the lion recognize his roar and respect the power of its owner. If they hear the roar, they know not to come any closer!

Our enemies also take notice when they hear us praising God. We're told, "The Sovereign LORD has spoken—so who can refuse to proclaim his message?" (Amos 3:8, NLT). When we raise our voices to express the majesty, grandeur, and sovereignty of our almighty God, we proclaim His holy name! Psalm 22:3 tells us that God sets up a throne in the praises of His people. In other words, the Lord resides in the presence of our praises!

If a lion can mark his territory with his mighty roar, just imagine what we can do with our praise! Do not permit anyone or anything to occupy your praise.

Your praise marks your territory.

THE POWER OF PRAISE

I suspect David recognized the importance of praise, because it's clearly integral to so many if not all of his psalms. But I also notice that before he defeated Goliath, David made it clear why he was so upset about the Philistine giant's attitude toward the Israelites and their God: Goliath enjoyed defying Israel and mocking the power of the One they worshipped. "Who is this uncircumcised Philistine that he should defy the armies of the living God?" David asked (1 Sam. 17:26).

Even before Goliath entered the scene, we're given an important clue about his tribe's irreverent intrusion into Jewish territory: "Now the Philistines gathered their forces for war and assembled at Sokoh in Judah" (1 Sam. 17:1). As we know, Judah means "praise," so therefore it's clear that the enemy at least symbolically, if not literally, violated sacred ground and blocked the praise of God's people.

> I cannot repeat this fact enough: the enemy wants to occupy your praise!
>
> He begins to defeat you the moment he takes hold of your worship.
>
> If he can interrupt your worship, then warfare immediately tilts in his favor.
>
> The enemies of truth, love, grace, and hope always attack your worship first.

They know that it's your power source, the conduit of confidence that keeps your reliance on God's power front and center. If they can bully, belittle, or bedevil you enough to disrupt your praise and worship, then they have temporarily severed your fuel line. This is why it's so important to keep the enemy out of your heart, your center of worship!

> Do not permit failure to occupy your praise.
>
> Do not permit fear to occupy your praise.
>
> Do not permit anxiety to occupy your praise.
>
> Do not permit depression, disappointment, or disease to occupy your praise!

The moment you recognize the enemy's tempting voice, you must not hesitate to roar with God's praises. Tell the enemy, "Get out of my Judah! You have no place here. You will not keep me from worshipping the Lord! You will not stop me from experiencing the health and wholeness God has for me!"

In the jungle, lions win the majority of their battles with their roar! The powerful sound commands the fear, respect, and recognition of those opposing them. The roar is intimidating. The roar makes enemies flee. The roar is the anthem of victory!

Right now you are fighting enemies in a stalemate instead of praising your way to a powerful victory. There are things you are fighting with that you should be praising through. Instead of cowering in fear before your foes like the Jewish army before Goliath, you must rush to the battle like David, praising God's power all the way.

During my visit to South Africa, I discovered the following: wounded lions still roar, tired lions still roar, and hungry lions still roar. In other words, you don't have to be happy to praise. You don't have to be perfect to praise. You don't have to be strong to praise. Even when you're weak, your roar prompts your enemies to flee.

> Have you ever praised and worshipped God even when your flesh said no?
>
> Have you ever praised and worshipped God in the midst of the storm?
>
> Have you ever praised and worshipped God in the shadow of a giant?

No matter how broken you may be, no matter how many wounds you have sustained, no matter how weak you feel, you still have the power to choose to praise and worship the living God. The coronavirus may have turned your world upside down, but it cannot silence your praise unless you let it.

Many people have shared with me that during the weeks and months when we were quarantined and sheltering-in-place, they relied on worship more than ever to sustain them. They sang praise songs out loud, tuned in to our online worship services, connected with other believers online, and prayed daily— sometimes hourly—to the only One worthy of our praise and worship. When uncertainty was the only certainty and the only thing unchanging was change, followers of Jesus roared out their praise.

It's not easy to celebrate the goodness of God when you can't see it the way you want. It's not logical to praise and worship Him when so many people are suffering, dying, grieving, and groaning. It's not rational to a world relying on human powers to stop an unseen enemy like the coronavirus.

Followers of Jesus, however, know that this is when we must exercise our faith muscles. This is when we yell out in confidence despite the pain we feel or the suffering we must endure. Even when we cry out in pain, we keep our trust in God as a constant, knowing He will work all things together for our good. With the humility and confidence of Job, someone who knew more than his fair share about suffering, we roar, "Though he slay me, yet will I trust in him" (Job 13:15, KJV).

Our scars remind us that God is faithful and will empower us to heal and experience the fullness of His love, joy, and peace. With the psalmist we declare, "You turned my wailing into dancing; you removed my sackcloth and clothed me with joy, that my heart may sing your praises and not be silent. LORD my God, I will praise you forever" (Ps. 30:11–12).

RECOGNIZE THE ROAR

When we roar like the Lion of Judah, we not only praise but we also sound the alarm for our loved ones. We announce to the world that we will not be silenced! We amplify our praise because of the hardships we experience rather than allow them to reduce our voices to whispers. When we are fighting to live healthy lives, our roar also becomes a clarion call to those around us. Our family, friends, neighbors, coworkers, and other community members stop and take notice when they hear us giving God praise in the midst of their panic and the world's pandemonium.

They listen to us just as we listen to God. I remember when our children were small, my wife and I taught them to recognize the difference, both in our diction and our tone, when we called them to come to us. They learned that when we declared, "It's time to go—come on!" in a normal voice, they needed to stop what they were doing, whether in the yard or playground or classroom, and head toward Mom and Dad. When we lowered our tone and raised our volume, however, they knew it was *imperative*! They were either in danger or in trouble, or both!

Our heavenly Father want us to recognize His voice and follow His guidance with the same responsive obedience. We are His children and can trust Him above all others to provide, protect, and empower us. Jesus told His followers, "My sheep listen to my voice; I know them, and they follow me. I give them eternal life, and they shall never perish; no one will snatch them out of my hand" (John 10:27–28).

Describing Himself as the guardian of the flock here, Christ makes it clear that He leads and protects each and every one of His sheep with His limitless power and infinite love. At that time, just as in David's day, shepherds kept watch over their sheep, led them to greener pastures and fresh water sources, and protected them from bears and lions. The animals became conditioned to recognize the sound of their particular shepherd's voice, obeying only it and not the voice of another.

In addition to being the Good Shepherd, Jesus is also the Lion of Judah, as we've seen. Remarkably enough, when a lion roars in the wilderness, his family, and sometimes even the entire pride of lions in the area, come running. Whether his roar signals imminent danger in the area, the discovery of food or water, or simply that it's time to move on, the blast of fierce bass notes never goes ignored.

The same is true for us: "They will follow the Lord; he will roar like a lion. When he roars, his children will come trembling from the west" (Hosea 11:10). The prophetic imagery of Jesus the Lion roaring as His children return to Him also empowers us with the anointing to roar our children back to God, to praise our children back home. Your words, actions, and attitudes create a roar that your children will eventually hear and follow when they may have strayed. Scripture promises, "Train up a child in the way he should go, and when he is old he will not depart from it" (Prov. 22:6, NKJV).

So no matter how far from you—and from God—your children may seem, don't you dare give up on them! Instead use your praise, your shouts, your prayers, and your roar to command their attention until they return home. How do we know our children will come back from their prodigal ways? How can we have confidence that they will beat their addictions, find their purpose, get the job they're made for, experience God's amazing grace, and be healed of their afflictions? Because our praise said so!

Permit me to remind you, not only are your children coming back home—your children will not inherit your mistakes. Your children will inherit your legacy of faith! We are not doomed to pass along the family dysfunction, the addictions, the abuse, the painful secrets and silent anguish—we have been set free and healed by God's power and might! When we invest in the eternal things of God, we create a holy inheritance for generations to come: "A good man leaves an inheritance to his children's children" (Prov. 13:22, NKJV).

Your children will not inherit your sins.

Your children will inherit your blessings!

Your children will not experience what you have lost.

Your children will experience what you have found!

Your children will not wallow in your weaknesses.

Your children will thrive in the strength of God's power in your life!

Your children will not go without.

Your children will enjoy the abundance of the Lord!

Roar with all your might and bring them home!

HORIZONTAL LION, VERTICAL LAMB

Many times we may not feel like roaring, especially when we are waiting on the fulfillment of our complete healing. But we must not despair, because God is faithful and always present with us. Our pain and suffering does not go unnoticed but will be redeemed by the One who suffered and died so that we may be healed by His stripes and know eternal joy with Him in heaven. God's Word assures us, "I have told you these things so that in me you may have peace. You will have suffering in this world. Be courageous! I have conquered the world" (John 16:33, CSB).

When the Philistines occupied their praise, the Israelites retreated in fear—until David came along and said, "Enough! We don't have to endure this—we are God's people! The victory belongs to the Lord!" He knew that God was with him and would equip and empower him to defeat the most overwhelming, overpowering, overbearing enemy imaginable. When you're on God's side, then those who get in your way as you serve Him don't stand a chance!

When we're suffering the unimaginable, when we're hurting and cannot remember the last time we enjoyed a pain-free day, when our emotions weigh us down with the burdens and cares of those we love, when our relentless grief wants to swallow us whole, when our minds and bodies are overloaded and overstressed, that's when we announce to the world as well as ourselves: "I'm not giving up. I only have to touch the hem of my Savior's garment and be healed. I don't know how it will happen, but my battle belongs to the Lord! Think I can't go on and be healthy and whole again? I will not only survive—*I will thrive!*"

I learned another amazing fact about lions in the wild while visiting the nature preserve in South Africa: a lion with a scar has access to new territory. While it's easy to think of Scar, Simba's villainous uncle from *The Lion King*, most African lions usually end up scarred from their various territorial battles over the years. Whether fighting with other lions over boundary skirmishes or defending themselves from natural enemies such as hyenas and cheetahs, lions accumulate scars that tell a story about their battle history.

Even more striking, though, is the way these battle scars work in the lion's favor when he ventures into new areas. Apparently the more scars a lion has accrued, the more other animals perceive him as a fighter, a leader, a survivor. Consequently, they usually stay out of his way and let him have their territory!

Whether our battle scars are invisible or apparent to those around us every day, they tell a story of our lives. Just like lions we can also use them to our advantage—not to intimidate others with our bad reputation but to demonstrate how God is at work in our lives! Why are we so inspired, so moved, so jubilant when we see a Paralympian transcending her physical limitations to win a gold medal? Why do we want the down-trodden underdog to win his battle with racial injustice and triumph over those who demean him? Why is David's victory over Goliath so powerful even now, more than two thousand years later?

Because people who overcome impress us. Their tenacity, determination, hard work, and most of all their faith show us that we can keep going until we win our current battle. We can endure our present suffering and trust that God will use it for good in His divine wisdom and sovereignty. People with scars have been through some painful situations and endured some devastating losses, but they have not given up.

They know God has called them to get back on their feet so they can step out in faith and keep going.

They know there are giants to slay and new territories to be tamed.

They know God has something glorious in the works just ahead, and the best is yet to come.

They know they have taken God's promise to heart: "Take possession of the land and settle in it, because I have given it to you to occupy" (Num. 33:53, NLT).

Some of the most powerful prayer warriors I've ever met look meek and frail at first glance—but then I listened to them describe the battles they fought and how God met them in the shadow of Goliath, in the pages of a medical report, in the paragraphs of a lawsuit, in the sting of a betrayal, or in the overwhelming, impossible obstacle before them. They know how to pray like a lamb and praise like a lion!

Even as I've been writing this chapter, the world continues to change dramatically in order to contain and overcome the COVID-19 viral pandemic. Bodies have suffered and lives have been lost. Businesses have been shuttered and economies have slumped. Leaders as well as those they serve have been forced to face the unknown and uncertainty of tumultuous circumstances beyond their control. But through all the quarrels and quarantines, through the recovery and relapses, the losses and legacies, God has been at work!

You are a horizontal lion and a vertical lamb!

No matter what you're facing, God knows exactly where you are and what you're going through. He has not abandoned you and will never forsake you. You are His precious child, His beloved lamb, His beautiful creation. Jesus will never let you go! As the Good Shepherd He reminds us that we are never out of His grasp: "Suppose one of you has a hundred sheep and loses one of them. Doesn't he leave the ninety-nine in the open country and go after the lost sheep until he finds it? And when he finds it, he joyfully puts it on his shoulders and goes home" (Luke 15:4–6).

You have wept like a lamb.

Now it's time to roar like a lion!

You are experiencing the healing that enables you to experience true health.

When others doubt you, then leave no doubt about your message.

You are not only a survivor—you are a thriver!

ALIVE TO THRIVE

Reflect on the questions below, and then after considering your answers, spend some time before the Lord in prayer. Take time to consider what you've experienced in recent months and the past year that require God's healing touch as you experience restoration and health. Open your heart before Him as you share all that you've suffered to get to this point. Reveal all the past wounds. Uncover all your old scars. Invite God's Spirit to work in you, with you, and through you. Give Him praise for how He has sustained you and will continue to bless you with wholeness and health!

1. How would you define *healthy living*? What does *healthy* mean to you now? Why? Has your definition changed since experiencing the impact of the coronavirus? Why or why not?

2. What does it mean to you to be both lion and lamb? How do the two symbolize both your weaknesses and your strengths?

3. What do you want to praise God for as you consider how He has brought you to this point in your life? Which blessings are you especially grateful to experience right now?

Dear God, in light of all that's happened in the world recently, I admit that I've often felt frightened, anxious, and alone. I've struggled to understand what's going on in a world that seems upside down. Too many times I've worried and wondered rather than resting in Your arms and singing Your praises. Forgive me, Lord, for the times I have not trusted You fully, for the moments when I've given in to doubts and temptations. Infuse me with Your Spirit yet again as I feel Your power coursing through me and experience the abundant life You came to bring! Amen.

Chapter 5

HAPPY TO BE HERE—WALK
BY FAITH, NOT SIGHT

*We experience happiness when we trust God
as the source of our contentment.*

*As we learn to walk by faith and not by sight,
we discover the joyful power to persevere.*

IN THE WAKE of the pandemic and all its collateral damage
many of us assumed we would never be happy again. After
all, clearly our world has changed and we can never go back
to the way things were. In a classic case of proving an old
adage true, we didn't realize what we had until we lost it. Even
if we have not experienced the devastating loss and crippling
effects afflicting so many of our neighbors, we may feel guilty
for enjoying the blessings we have. We wonder how we can be
happy if so many others are hurting, suffering, grieving.

Now, as we move forward and shift from surviving to
thriving, it's a good time to rethink what true happiness is all
about. While countless books, seminars, retreats, programs,
and gurus want to share the secret to happiness with you,
there's a much simpler path: the one Jesus revealed during His
time on earth. In fact, Jesus came to earth and lived as a man
in order that you and I could be happy. His teachings provide

a foundation for true happiness, which He assumed was the desire of every man, woman, and child.

If this surprises you, then no wonder you've been unhappy!

REDEFINING HAPPY

In His teaching best known as the Sermon on the Mount, Christ starts with a series of statements that reveal a great deal about the essence of happiness. Usually called the Beatitudes, these declarations all begin with a blessing: "Blessed are the poor in spirit...blessed are the meek...blessed are the pure in heart..." and so on (Matt. 5:3–10). In just a little over one hundred words, Jesus uses the Greek word *makarios*, which usually gets translated as "blessed," nine times.[1]

Perhaps a more simple and direct translation of *makarios* is our word *happy*. Originally the Greeks coined their word in reference to the carefree, ethereal life enjoyed by their fabled gods of Greek mythology. At the time Jesus repeated it in His sermon, *makarios* was a word frequently used to describe the wealthy and well established, as opposed to the hardships endured by the poor and working class.

Before an audience of thousands of these very people, Jesus chose a word they would likely never use to describe themselves. They were surely shocked to hear this word applied to their situations. Counterintuitive and even illogical based on their experience, Jesus' message was that their suffering was not in vain, that their struggles were not futile endeavors. Surely it was shocking for them to hear:

Happy are the poor in spirit.

Happy are those who mourn.

Happy are the meek.

Happy are those who hunger and thirst for justice.

Happy are the merciful.

Happy are the pure in heart.

Happy are the peacemakers.

Happy are those who are persecuted for righteousness.

Happy are you when others revile you and utter false-
hoods against you...Rejoice and be glad (Matt. 5:3–12).

Simply put, Jesus revealed a stunning concept: *anyone could
be happy.*

Jesus was not promising pie-in-the-sky emotional highs
or cruel incentives to suffer in self-righteous silence. No, He
was sharing the essence of the gospel, the good news that
God's love and forgiveness extended to everyone, not just the
powerful, educated, wealthy, and famous. This news turned
the shame and contempt lobbied by the elite echelons into
badges of honor. Jesus contrasted the worldly kinds of happiness contingent on money, possessions, power, beauty,
sex appeal, and popularity with a kind that was permanent,
eternal, unchanging. The kind that would permit the apostle
Paul to say:

I have learned to be content whatever the circumstances.
I know what it is to be in need, and I know what it is
to have plenty. I have learned the secret of being content
in any and every situation, whether well fed or hungry,
whether living in plenty or in want. I can do all this
through him who gives me strength.
—Philippians 4:11–13

Christ claimed His followers would be known by their love. He told the crowds of people that they were blessed with happiness just as they were—without any of the worldly requisites. Jesus said He came to bring us a full, abundant life, one brimming with joy, peace, and contentment as we fulfill our God-given purpose. A happy life even in the midst of a pandemic, unemployment, economic recession, and the losses so many have endured. A happiness founded on the living hope of our faith in Him.

NEAR AND FAR

Experiencing the kind of happiness Jesus promised is no easier or harder now than it was when He first preached the Sermon on the Mount. It comes back once again to our basis of reference. Are we focused on what the world says will make us happy or on what God promises will provide happiness as a natural by-product of our passionate obedience to Him?

So much of our view of happiness relies on how we see life. As I've gotten older, I've had to rely on glasses and contact lenses to correct my vision and help me see with the 20/20 clarity my eyes cannot produce on their own. After enduring pain, trauma, and hardships, we may also need help seeing clearly in order to experience the happiness God has for us.

Being unable to see clearly manifests itself with our eyes. Spiritually impaired vision, however, can often be more difficult to diagnose. I suspect that many of us, both in our lives and in our relationships with God, suffer from myopia or hyperopia as well. Some people have difficulty seeing beyond what's in front of them and tend to live only for today. They lose sight of the bigger picture of God's eternal panorama because their future seems so blurry and uncertain. They're not sure where they're going from one season to the next because they can't sense the things of God with clarity and certainty.

Many others struggle with the opposite problem: They're always looking behind or ahead but do not appreciate, honor, and respect what's right in front of them. They stay distracted from engaging with the present and often end up paralyzed by past regrets and future worries. Their spiritual farsightedness prevents them from experiencing the abundant blessings God has already bestowed upon them because they're inclined to think the grass must be greener, either through the rose-colored glasses of romantic nostalgia for the past or the amber-tinted, polarized sunglasses looking ahead at the next perceived bright horizon.

The challenge to maintaining clear spiritual vision is often personal pride and ego, both our own as well as the self-interests of others. David faced this challenge head-on when forced to interact with King Saul, the reigning leader anointed by God over Israel. You'll recall the prophet Samuel expressed his fear of Saul to God after the Lord directed Samuel to go to Bethlehem and anoint God's next chosen king, David (1 Sam. 16:2). God had established Saul as the first king of Israel (1 Sam. 9) but later revealed His disappointment to Samuel after Saul disobeyed God (1 Sam. 15:10–11).

God allowed Saul to continue to rule even as David matured and gained experience as a leader. With David's selection and anointing as Saul's successor, however, the dynamic between the two leaders, one ascending and the other descending, was naturally tense. The modern term "frenemy" comes to mind to describe the unique blend of Saul's jealousy, David's respect, and the transition of Israel's throne from the elder to the younger. Their relationship was further complicated by the fact that David became best friends with Saul's son Jonathan and married Saul's daughter Michal.

Even before Saul knew that David would replace him as

king, he tried to force David to follow in the older leader's methods. When young David visited the battlefront between the Hebrews and Philistines, learned of Goliath's sacrilege, and decided to fight the giant, no one took David seriously. Who was this kid showing up on the scene and thinking he could accomplish what an entire army had not been able to achieve? By accepting Goliath's challenge, David was showing up not only his older brothers but the entire Israelite army!

What others viewed as insurmountable, David viewed as an opportunity for God's power and glory to be displayed. Despite his youth and inexperience, David's faith in God was taller, stronger, and more confident than the muscles, mockery, and might of any foe. While others tried to force David to recognize the impossibility of winning this battle, he knew he would not only survive the battle—relying on God's power, he would thrive!

JAWS OF DEFEAT

As if attempting to help the overzealous young shepherd to think clearly, King Saul offered an obvious and patronizing response: "You are not able to go out against this Philistine and fight him; you are only a young man, and he has been a warrior from his youth" (1 Sam. 17:33). His was the voice of reason; a leader's wisdom based on logic; a military strategist's assessment based on size, strength, and resources; a king unwilling to lose face.

Instead of seeing what Saul considered obvious, however, David saw the way his past trials and triumphs had prepared him for this challenge:

> But David said to Saul, "Your servant has been keeping his father's sheep. When a lion or a bear came and carried off a sheep from the flock, I went after it, struck it

and rescued the sheep from its mouth. When it turned on me, I seized it by its hair, struck it and killed it. Your servant has killed both the lion and the bear; this uncircumcised Philistine will be like one of them, because he has defied the armies of the living God. The LORD who rescued me from the paw of the lion and the paw of the bear will rescue me from the hand of this Philistine."

Saul said to David, "Go, and the LORD be with you."

—1 SAMUEL 17:34–37

From David's vantage point he was not without the experience necessary to defeat Goliath. As a shepherd responsible for his family's flock, David had to protect his sheep from natural predators such as lions and bears, formidable adversaries no matter who goes up against them. The fact that these wild beasts had been defeated just as they were about to munch some mutton is indeed remarkable! David literally pried his precious sheep away from the jaws of defeat, and he seized the angry predator by its hair and killed it. He viewed Goliath as just another adversary to be slain, no greater than a lion or bear no matter how big, strong, or experienced.

But this pernicious Philistine had God's reputation in his jaws, a theft David could not ignore. With the stakes so much higher, David knew that if God had protected him on the rolling hillsides from attacks by bears and lions, then God would surely protect him now. Rather than trivializing his past experience or minimizing his victories, David used them to bolster his confident faith in God.

When you're facing overwhelming odds and up against what everyone else considers impossible, how do you respond?

Do you feel a surge of confidence because you remember the many times God has empowered you to win the battle and snatch victory from the jaws of defeat? Or do you assume that this new obstacle is bigger, stronger, and scarier than anything you've faced before? Each time we endure a trying time, each day we push through what feels unbearable, each moment we surrender our control and rely on God's power and provision, we slay our own bears and lions. Every time we experience His protection, we are preparing for the time when Goliath might cross our path. We're exercising our spiritual muscle and stepping out in faith for the time when others tell us we can't conquer the giant blocking our path.

With each bear and lion we conquer, we're surviving in order to thrive.

STICKS AND STONES

After David gave his rebuttal to Saul's warning, the king must have realized that he was never going to deter this young man's fighting spirit. Like someone resigned to seeing another fail after being cautioned, Saul told David, "Go, and the LORD be with you" (1 Sam. 17:37). Can't you just hear him sigh? Perhaps see him raise his eyebrows or roll his eyes to express his resignation? Can't you just imagine Saul thinking, "Poor thing! So naïve—this kid has no idea what and who he's up against! Off to be slaughtered by Goliath, thinking his faith is enough to overcome an enemy that large."

Others will often warn us, caution us, and flat-out forbid us from entering the battle God has called us to fight. Their advice may be well intended or covertly sarcastic. They may pity us, patronize us, or penalize us, but their warnings must never stop us from doing what we know God wants us to do. Their logic may be sound, their reasons well thought out, and their forecast probable. It doesn't matter, though, when we fight the enemy of God! When we go to battle against injustice, against fear, against poverty, against sickness, against intolerance and prejudice, we must never let the contagious caution of others infect our spirits.

Sometimes those who warn us will go one step further and try to help us. They realize they can't prevent us from facing the giant, so they assume we need their power and protection. Or perhaps they simply want to absolve themselves of the potential guilt they anticipate feeling when and if we fail. This was apparently the case with Saul and the young shepherd turned soldier. Even if the king believed David to be foolish and immature in his determination to fight the Philistine, the leader still felt responsible for helping this would-be hero. If he couldn't stop David, the least he could do was equip the young man to the best of his royal ability:

> Then Saul dressed David in his own tunic. He put a coat of armor on him and a bronze helmet on his head. David fastened on his sword over the tunic and tried walking around, because he was not used to them.
> "I cannot go in these," he said to Saul, "because I am not used to them." So he took them off. Then he took his staff in his hand, chose five smooth stones from the stream, put them in the pouch of his shepherd's bag and, with his sling in his hand, approached the Philistine.
> —1 SAMUEL 17:38–40

Now, offering one of his subjects his own coat of armor and weaponry was no small gesture on Saul's part. The king's protection befit his importance and was therefore often thicker and heavier than the armor worn by an average soldier. Although Saul had actively engaged with his men in battle, his sword and shield may have been more elaborate, ceremonial, and decorative than practical. Notice that Saul did not merely offer his armor and weapons to David—he actually dressed David in his royal tunic and coat of arms.

Keep in mind, too, that because Saul was king, there was

really no way for David to refuse such a dramatic gesture. The king was God's chosen leader, so David at least needed to show respect, which he did by trying on Saul's tunic, armor, and sword. But like a little boy playing dress up in his father's clothes, David found the uniform cumbersome and ultimately restrictive. He balked and said something that in itself required courage: "I can't wear these—they're not what I'm used to!"

David turned down the king's attempt to help him because he knew the Lord would use his past victories to vanquish this present adversary. Intuitively, I suspect, as well as through his spiritual relationship with God, David knew a fundamental principle of holy leadership: what protects and empowers one leader does not necessarily transfer to his or her successor! Saul's intentions seem honorable enough. After all, what kind of king would let a teenager from the backwoods beyond Bethlehem take on a human fighting machine like Goliath? But Saul's attempt to help David makes the contrast between human power and divine power, between circumstantial confidence and foundational faith, that much clearer.

Because his trust was in the Lord, David relied on what he knew best, the same tools and weapons he used to overcome bears and lions with God's help: "Then he took his staff in his hand, chose five smooth stones from the stream, put them in the pouch of his shepherd's bag and, with his sling in his hand, approached the Philistine" (1 Sam. 17:40). It didn't matter how thick the king's armor was or how sharp his sword—they slowed David down and impeded his ability to fight the way God had prepared him to fight.

Can you imagine this scene? Something about it strikes me as funny, almost like a farce, because the contrast is so stunning. The mighty king is afraid to face the bully in battle, but a fresh-faced young shepherd is not. The leader of the army gives the finest armor and weapons available—his own—to the determined underdog, who rejects them and instead chooses sticks and stones, his shepherd's staff, and worn-smooth rocks from the riverbed. David used what he had, what he knew comfortably, what had worked before—no matter how it appeared to those watching.

QUIET THE GIANT

Just consider what Goliath and the Philistines must have thought when this hyped-up Hebrew kid plunged his hand into the water and pulled up rocks! Or how foolish David must have looked clutching his shepherd's staff with its curved crook to gather stray sheep. The giant, in fact, said to David, "Am I a dog, that you come at me with sticks?" (1 Sam. 17:43). The mighty warrior apparently felt insulted that David was so foolish and/or arrogant not to prepare more strategically. "And the Philistine cursed David by his gods. 'Come here,' he said, 'and I'll give your flesh to the birds and wild animals!'" (1 Sam. 17:43–44).

David was not intimidated or afraid, however. His response to Goliath reveals a very different way of seeing their confrontation:

> David said to the Philistine, "You come against me with sword and spear and javelin, but I come against you in the name of the LORD Almighty, the God of the armies of Israel, whom you have defied. This day the LORD will deliver you into my hands, and I'll strike you down and cut off your head. This very day I will give the carcasses of the Philistine army to the birds and the wild animals, and the whole world will know that there is a God in Israel. All those gathered here will know that it is not by sword or spear that the LORD saves; for the battle is the LORD's, and he will give all of you into our hands."
>
> —1 SAMUEL 17:45–47

No weapon in this world is a match for the supernatural power of the living God! While Goliath cursed and mocked his opponent, David spoke objective, prophetic truth—"for the battle is the LORD's"—about the spiritual reality of their situation. The carnage David then described had nothing to do with his own power, acumen, or skill as a warrior and everything to do with the glory, power, and honor of the Lord Almighty! Goliath's confidence was the result of his own power, strength, and contempt for his opponents and their God. Goliath relied on swords and spears, metal and wood to fight, but David relied on faith.

If we trust in God to save us from the power of sin and death, then we can trust Him to save us from the giants coming at us with their weapons of anger, fear, addiction, debt, intolerance, injustice, and inequality. Our happiness resides in our relationship with Him. Only when we attempt to fight these battles in our own power do we limit our access to the limitless power of God. Only when we put our faith in weapons and shields of our own making do we set ourselves up for failure. Only when we cower to the curses of our enemies rather than courageously speak God's truth do we falter. The writer of Ephesians expressed the essence of David's experience this way: "For our struggle is not against flesh and blood, but against the rulers, against the authorities, against the powers of this dark world and against the spiritual forces of evil in the heavenly realms" (Eph. 6:12).

Too often we view the battles we face through the limitations of our mortal eyes. We see the outward appearance of what's going on around us even as God sees all that's inside our hearts. We're tempted to put our happiness in money, weapons, beauty, experience, relationships, achievements, accolades, and authorities. This power struggle will never be a fair one, or even close to being evenly matched, because nothing in this life, nothing on this earth can stand up to the limitless power of our sovereign almighty God! "If God is for us, who can be against us? He who did not spare his own Son, but gave him up for us all—how will he not also, along with him, graciously give us all things?" (Rom. 8:31–32).

What battle have you been trying to fight in your own power with weapons of your own making? What conflicts have been clouding your ability to see how God has already equipped you to defeat the giants in your life? Whose armor have you been wearing, fully aware that it limits your ability to fight with the freedom you have in the Spirit? Whose weapon have you been borrowing instead of using what is already in your hand?

If you want to experience the limitless life of God's abundant peace, power, and purpose, then it's time to lay down everything that's in your way. If you want to live a life of victory over victimhood and quiet the giant voices cluttering your consciousness, then your battle must belong to the Lord. If you want happiness sewn from a garment of peace and stitched by joy, then rely on God. Because as Goliath found out the hard way, God always has the final word!

FACE THE FIGHT

As we all know, underdog David defeated giant Goliath. The actual battle sequence must have seemed anticlimactic, a letdown from the adrenaline-fueled, action-packed, life-or-death fight to the finish that spectators on both sides likely anticipated:

> As the Philistine moved closer to attack him, David ran quickly toward the battle line to meet him. Reaching into his bag and taking out a stone, he slung it and struck the Philistine on the forehead. The stone sank into his forehead, and he fell facedown on the ground. So David triumphed over the Philistine with a sling and a stone;

without a sword in his hand he struck down the Philistine
and killed him.

—1 SAMUEL 17:48–50

Notice David didn't hesitate or delay in facing his opponent
head-on. Goliath was probably used to intimidating his opponents enough that he no longer even relied on his strength
or skill. He had mastered the art of being a blowhard bully
and spent the past forty days performing daily for those who
revered him. Perhaps Goliath thought David's bravado would
crumble once the youth felt the presence of his nearly ten-foot
frame tower over him. Maybe Goliath thought all his taunts,
threats, and curses would get inside David's head enough
to undermine his confidence and erode his courage. The
Philistine giant may have even expected to simply slaughter
the young Hebrew shepherd with a single blow.

> Whatever strategy or expectation Goliath had really
> didn't matter.
>
> Because the battle belonged to the Lord.
>
> David ran quickly toward the battle line to meet him.
>
> No backing down, no running away, no compromise.

Sometimes I worry that many of us spend so much time
getting ready to fight that we delay actually fighting the giants
God wants us to slay. Instead of running quickly to the confrontation, we take our time and wander around. We may even
do this under the guise of waiting patiently on God. Instead
of a bold declaration, our refrain becomes a tentative question. We settle for surviving instead of thriving. Instead of
running quickly into the battle with faith-fueled confidence,
we let doubt derail our determination. We start listening to

the enemy and allowing him to plant seeds of uncertainty, fear, and distrust in our thinking.

While there are certainly times we're called to wait upon the Lord, we should never use this as our excuse when we know we're called to battle with the giant blocking our path. Never delay when it's time to slay! Don't postpone admitting you need help. Don't waste time wondering if now is the time to quit the habit holding you hostage. Don't procrastinate or prevaricate when it's time to eradicate! Empowered by God, you can fight with confidence and overcome the giant blocking your path.

Don't strive to survive when you can thrive!

BATTLE LINES

David used his slingshot, a simple tool from his boyhood as a shepherd, to bring down someone almost twice his size. He did what no one thought could be done, least of all by an inexperienced teenager without armor or a sword. David fought for the Lord and drew on divine power. He viewed himself as a humble conduit of God's will and the divine power required to fulfill that will.

Goliath, on the other hand, fought for himself and drew on his own strength. With such a size and reputation, this giant warrior wasn't fighting for his comrades, his tribe, or his kinsmen. He was fighting for sport, for the sheer thrill of displaying his ability and basking in the admiration of others. His pride blinded him to the possibility that any Israelite could defeat him, certainly not an untrained kid with a handful of rocks.

His arrogance illustrates the adage that pride goes before a fall. When we think we've insulated ourselves against calamity, protected ourselves against disaster, promoted ourselves to ensure celebrity, and empowered ourselves enough to always win, then we may win for a while. We may think we're on top of the world as we step on others to become king of the hill or queen of the castle. But the battle belongs to the Lord.

> The *Titanic* was supposedly unsinkable, yet it hit an iceberg and sank on its maiden voyage.

> Unbeatable sports teams lose championships against underdogs with terrible records.

> Tycoons go bankrupt, and beauty queens grow old.

If we rely on anything other than God as our power source, we may cast a giant shadow for a while, but ultimately, like Goliath, we will fall. Pride is not limited to being a braggart or conceited. When you think your gift will take you further than God's grace, your destiny dies. Anytime you think you've made it this far in life because of your gifts, abilities, intelligence, skills, acumen, determination, drive, contacts, or courage, then you are sadly mistaken. Whether you realize it now or not, hell has plotted to take you out many times, and only God has stood between you and the destructive schemes of the enemy.

> When you attempt to occupy someone else's armor, your ability to fight suffers.

> When you rely on human weapons and material possession, you lose your battles.

> When your cause elevates you instead of Yahweh, you will fall.

> When you make happiness the point, you will never be happy.

Every time you think that what you have is bigger than what God has, your pride defeats you. Every time you think that your sin is beyond God's forgiveness, your pride blinds you. Every time you worry rather than keep your faith, your sense of control grows stronger. Pride is anything that causes you to cling to your own abilities instead of surrendering to God's power. Simply put, pride = YOU > GOD!

In order to slay the giants in our lives, we must remain humble. Scripture tells us that "God opposes the proud but shows favor to the humble" (Prov. 3:34; Jas. 4:6) and "For those who exalt themselves will be humbled, and those who humble themselves will be exalted" (Luke 14:11, NLT). Humility is the wineskin that best manages the wine of God's favor. When you step out in faith with humility, you can expect God to do great things—that which others perceive as impossible. You don't need thicker armor or sharper weapons, more time or a larger team.

You simply need faith.

SLAY YOUR GIANT

While others ran in fear, David ran toward the front line because he knew the battle belonged to the Lord. While Saul tried to figure out what to do, David knew what had to be done. While Goliath bragged and boasted, David trusted God for the outcome.

When giants block your path, it's hard to see beyond them.

Giants make you nearsighted so that you struggle to see what's on the other side. They draw battle lines that block your view. There are things you cannot see until other things get out of the way! The giants you slay today determine the path you walk tomorrow.

Is there a Goliath taunting you in the corners of your mind, calling you names and reminding you of past defeats? Planting seeds of doubt about who God is and all that He has for you?

Is there something ruling over you that impedes you from seeing everything that God has for you? Something that prevents you from seeing your future, from clearly seeing the way forward? Maybe you can't see beyond your level of debt and the student loans that weigh you down. Perhaps you can't see beyond the medical report. It might be the glass ceiling in your workplace or the limitations of a relationship. You may not be able to see beyond the demands of your family or the wounds of your past. No matter how hard you try, you can't see beyond these giants in your life and the looming shadows they cast over your future.

But the battle belongs to the Lord, my friend.

David was told he would never defeat Goliath, and he did.

Maybe it's time for you to enter the battle and defeat the impossible giant before you.

What giant are you about to slay? Is there a construct, a wound, a sin, a thought, an attitude, a language, a relationship, a sentiment, a doubt, or an inability to forgive that taunts you and wants to destroy you? Is there anything impeding your ability to see the grace, glory, truth, love, and power of Jesus Christ in you, with you, for you, and through you?

Kill that giant!

Let your Goliath fall.

When your past dies, God's future for you lives!

When defeat dies, victory lives.

When hate dies, love lives.

When chaos dies, shalom lives.

When the nightmare dies, the dream lives.

When strife dies, unity lives.

When sorrow dies, joy lives!

I am here to declare by faith that this is the hour, this is the moment that your addiction dies forever more. Your fear no longer has power over you. Your depression cannot consume you. Your past abuse will not haunt you.

Shame dies today.

Condemnation dies today.

Depression dies today.

Anxiety dies today.

Generational curses die today.

Sexual immorality dies today.

Witchcraft and idolatry die today.

Every lie of the enemy upon your life dies today.

The battle belongs to the Lord!

Let giant pride die.

Let arrogance die.

Let jealousy die.

Let unbelief die.

Let unforgiveness die.

Let the old way of thinking die.

Let the old way of talking die.

I can understand if you doubt me, but do not doubt the truth of God's Word! The battle belongs to the Lord, and Christ Jesus won the victory for us all when He defeated sin and death on the cross. By the power of His Spirit we have the stones of faith to kill the giants in our path! We're assured, "Those who belong to Christ Jesus have nailed the passions and desires of their sinful nature to his cross and crucified them there" (Gal. 5:24, NLT).

David faced what everyone else viewed as an undefeatable foe. He made it clear that this battle was about obedience and about holiness. He trusted God and killed the giant that wanted to destroy him. When others told David he would never win, when they forced him into roles that did not fit, when they tried to tell him how to do what they themselves could not do, he faced his foe and won. You have the same power available to you today. You are not without hope. You deserve to be happy because God made you to experience the fullness of His joy.

It's time to reclaim happiness as your heavenly birthright!

ALIVE TO THRIVE

Once again, use the following questions to help you reflect on this chapter's message and apply it to your own life. While it's not required, I encourage you to write down your responses so you can refer back to them later. After you've spent a few moments thinking about your answers to these questions, go to the Lord in prayer and share with Him the giants looming in your heart. As before, a short prayer is included to help you get started, but make it your own as you talk to your Father.

1. What giants are presently blocking your view and preventing you from experiencing the happiness God has for you? How can you surrender this battle to the Lord and trust Him for your victory?

2. Do you believe God wants you to be happy? Why or why not? How did you form the beliefs that shape your response? How does a biblical definition of happiness change the way you think about it?

3. When has your pride prevented you from seeing clearly and relying on God as the source of your joy and happiness? How can you trust Him to help you defeat the giants looming over you?

Lord, forgive me for often making my happiness conditional on worldly things. I know that You are the only source of abiding joy and the contentment that comes from living an abundant, happy life. I want to trust You and recognize how You have already equipped me with everything I need to defeat the giants I'm now facing. Give me Your power and perspective as I seek to move forward and see clearly. Thank You for providing all I need to fulfill the purpose to which You have called me. I praise You for not only giving me life but wanting me to thrive! Amen.

Chapter 6

HUMBLE PIE—SERVE BEFORE YOU SLICE

Our pride may help us survive,
but it becomes an obstacle when we want to thrive.

Only when you put others before yourself can you
discover the joy of a servant's heart.

T HE COVID-19 PANDEMIC brought our world to its knees. Events were cancelled, no matter how large or small, how elaborate or simple, how important or frivolous. From conventions to church picnics, bar mitzvahs to sports bars, concerts to campouts, Broadway to Hollywood, groups and gatherings could not be risked if we wanted to avoid exposure and prevent contagion. We were all forced to change our lifestyles in dramatic ways, whether this meant working from home, shopping online, cancelling vacations, or improvising ways to remain connected.

From those considered powerful to the most impoverished, the novel coronavirus made us all equals. US Congress and British Parliament, and most governing bodies around the world, had no choice but to end sessions and temporarily close their doors. Not just one team or one league but entire seasons of professional sports—basketball, hockey, baseball, and soccer, to name a few—were cancelled, postponed, or dramatically shortened. International borders closed in an attempt to curtail transmission of the virus, effectively halting travel, tourism, and hospitality industries.

Billion-dollar corporations ceased production as millions of workers lost their jobs and primary income sources. The only industry thriving was the medical and health-care field, which was stretched to capacity and beyond by demand for those battling the coronavirus. Schools and universities shuttered classrooms and campuses, resorting instead to online education. Entertainment venues, once home to performances by renowned icons, could no longer safely host the crowds of fans often numbering in the thousands. Films and TV productions went on hiatus, switching to live broadcasts sent from living rooms, home offices, and makeshift basement studios. Nothing escaped the impact of the pandemic.

Many of us struggled to understand how this could happen. Most of us who live in the twenty-first century had never experienced anything like it and had imagined such a scenario only on film screens and in the pages of fiction. How could such a virus resist the analysis of our most brilliant scientists and doctors trying to develop a vaccine? How could government policies and national measures defy containment? Surely with all of our advanced technology, online resources, and pharmaceutical innovation we had evolved beyond the deadly grasp of something so tiny and invisible to the unaided eye.

After all, we do not live in our ancestors' world of influenza, polio, smallpox, and measles. With such deadly immune assailants vanquished, many of us believed we would see the cure for cancer revealed in our lifetime. Chemical treatments, vaccinations, diagnostic technology, and medication breakthroughs have extended our life expectancy by years over what our grandparents and great-grandparents experienced. In developed countries such as the United States the majority of us enjoy clean water, an abundant food supply, and homes adequate to shelter us from seasonal elements and vacillating temperatures.

Millions of citizens have enjoyed advancements and inventions only imagined by previous generations: smartphones and flat-screen TVs, microwaves and temperature control systems, cars that park themselves and security cameras that record every visitor. The temptation for those blessed by such luxuries to overlook the needs of others, to rely on automation, and to feel entitled to such convenience and control often felt too great. Pride seeped in the edges of our modern lives without us realizing the depth of its permeation.

Then in a matter of minutes, hours, days, and weeks we realized how much we took for granted. Like something out of my beloved *Star Trek* universe or the imagination of fantasy, science fiction, and horror novelists, the global village became a ghost town. For all our technology, money, power, and assumed control over every aspect of modern life, nothing could stop something we could not even see.

Everyone was vulnerable.

THE PATH OF PRIDE

Changes, losses, and deficits resulting from the coronavirus pandemic forced us to confront our pride. We watched our ability to control events, other people, and even nature itself crumble in the wake of something beyond our understanding and containment. Whatever power we thought we possessed, and whatever our basis for it, evaporated in the scorching reality of a lethal virus unleashed. We could not protect and defend ourselves against an unknown, silent biological assailant.

Pride is a coin with two sides.

It used to have mostly negative connotations: Pride goes before a fall. Pride and prejudice. Swallow your pride. Take pride in your work. These timeworn sayings assume that pride is to be avoided and cannot sustain itself because of its basis. Pride inflates our thoughts and feelings and reorients the world until we are at the center of everything. We assume that we must base our self-worth on something other than our intrinsic identity as God's creation made in His divine image. As C. S. Lewis observed in *Mere Christianity*, "Pride leads to every other vice: it is the complete anti-God state of mind."[1]

Consider that insight for just a moment: *every sinful struggle you experience can be traced back to pride.* The path of pride leads to destruction.

Instead of recognizing God's holy power and inherent goodness, we rely on our physical strength and attractive appearance, our wealth and status symbols, our education and achievements, the power we wield and the offices we hold. We probably don't consider ourselves to be like Goliath, the champion of the Philistine army taunting and towering over the Israelites, but our self-reliance is much the same.

We grow accustomed to having most of what we want the way we want it. We try to exercise control over the areas of life tied to our comfort, convenience, and identity. We compare and compete, both privately as we scroll with envy on social media and then publicly when we post our own carefully curated images and words in retaliation.

Goliath didn't have Facebook, Twitter, or Instagram to amplify his pride, but his voice echoed with arrogant confidence nonetheless. He had been blessed with the enormous advantage of exceptional height, physical size, and bodily strength. The giant had apparently maximized those physical gifts by exercising his body as both a bully and a soldier. Goliath was literally ten feet tall and weighed more than two average-sized men, so it's easy to see why he learned to rely on his size, strength, and reputation.

It seems likely, though, that by the time David encountered

Goliath, the warrior was fighting for his own sporting reputation more than the cause of his tribe. He clearly enjoyed
baiting the Israelites and lording his physical power over them.
No wonder then that he can't fathom how a teenaged shepherd boy—a messenger sent from home who was not even old
enough to be conscripted yet—would dare accept Goliath's
challenge.

"Am I a dog, that you come at me with sticks?" asked the
Philistine, seeing the boy wielded only a shepherd's staff and a
leather pouch. (1 Sam. 17:43). Why, it was insulting for anyone
to be so naïve that he would approach Goliath without max-
imum preparation. Then all the more enjoyable it would be, the
giant probably thought, to tear the insolent youth limb from
limb: "And the Philistine cursed David by his gods. 'Come
here,' he said, 'and I'll give your flesh to the birds and the wild
animals!'" (1 Sam. 17:43–44).

I can't help but wonder if Goliath ever realized the tables
were turning. When David carefully placed the smooth river
stone in the homemade slingshot? When the stone soared
toward his head like a bullet? Perhaps the giant died not realizing what had happened to him, but I suspect there was a
moment of reckoning when he realized he was not invincible
after all. In an upset of historic, epic proportions, David beat
all the odds and toppled an unbeatable foe more than twice
his size.

It's tempting to identify with David, and as those who trust
in the God of the impossible, we should. The shepherd boy was
overlooked by his family when the Lord's prophet, Samuel, followed divine direction and came to his home to anoint the
next king of Israel. Chosen and anointed, David still had to
wait before taking the throne. He still had lessons to learn, and
Saul had not yet lost the crown. Demonstrating his courage
and bedrock faith in God's power, David was first dismissed as
foolish, unaware, and unprepared to become the giant slayer.

When Saul was unable to persuade David to abandon his showdown, the king tried to help by equipping the young man with royal armor and weaponry.

David knew better than to place his trust in shields and blades, however. He wasn't blind to the enormous obstacle blocking not only his path but the path of his people. The future king knew the battle belonged to the Lord. David only had to do what he knew to do. He didn't know how to wield a heavy sword in clunky, even heavier armor. He didn't have the experience of being a soldier, which everyone around him assumed must be the primary prerequisite for defeating the giant. Instead David used what he had—his courage and resourcefulness, his experience protecting his flock from bears and lions.

Most of all, David reflected humility. His attitude of faith-based power and selflessness contrasts sharply with Goliath's boastful, self-reliant pride. David did not want to kill the giant so that he could show up his brothers, the other soldiers, or King Saul. David did not want to defeat Goliath so that others would see him as a larger-than-life hero, their next royal leader. David did not even kill the Philistine to uphold Israel.

> David killed Goliath in the name of the Lord, by His power and for His glory.

> David not only survived his encounter with a seemingly impossible obstacle, he thrived.

> David thrived because he served the Lord.

> Service is a hallmark of humility.

LESSON FROM LIMITATIONS

When the basis of our security, power, and stability is suddenly shaken, we have a choice to make. We can dig in and fight harder to regain what we've lost, letting our anger, pain, and sorrow fuel our attempts to move forward. Whether we become more conservative in our strategies or take greater risks, when we focus on regaining what we've lost through our own power, we only compound our losses. Instead of learning the lesson of our limitations and being humbled, we once again rely on human powers and earthly devices.

In the midst of crisis, when we experience loss, as unimaginable devastation engulfs us, we have an opportunity. This is true not only in times of pandemic, recession, and social unrest but really at any time in our lives. When we're grounded involuntarily, we're tempted to despair. When we remain grounded by humility, we trust in the Lord. We have no pride, no hope, and no resources except through Him. When we're forced to our knees by life's blows, we struggle to get up. When we choose to fall on our knees in prayer and worship before our mighty God, then He lifts us up.

Those of us committed to following Jesus always try to obey God and receive power from His Spirit, but when our usual routines and systems are turned inside out, many of us realize we were not trusting the Lord as completely as we could. In those moments when we have nothing and nowhere else to turn, we realize how our self-righteousness has become an idol. Rather than maintaining a posture of gratitude, stewardship, and humility, we allow our egos to eclipse our souls.

We begin thinking we are better than other people because we obey God and seek His ways. We read our Bibles and volunteer at local shelters, attend church regularly and lead small groups. The irony, of course, is that we become just as legalistic, hypocritical, and self-righteous as the religious leaders in

Jesus' time. They were so consumed by their own importance that they lost sight of the parallel humanity they shared with all people. They were so devoted to their religion that they did not leave room for the Son of God when He appeared as a man before them.

Christ didn't hesitate to call them out on their prideful self-righteousness either. He repeatedly confronted them for emphasizing their appearance in front of others rather than the state of their hearts before God. Jesus called the Pharisees and Sadducees vipers and whitewashed tombs, poisonous and hard hearted despite efforts to appear otherwise. In one particular parable He compared the faith of a religious leader with that of a tax collector, someone despised by all:

> To some who were confident of their own righteousness and looked down on everyone else, Jesus told this parable: "Two men went up to the temple to pray, one a Pharisee and the other a tax collector. The Pharisee stood by himself and prayed: 'God, I thank you that I am not like other people—robbers, evildoers, adulterers—or even like this tax collector. I fast twice a week and give a tenth of all I get.'
>
> "But the tax collector stood at a distance. He would not even look up to heaven, but beat his breast and said, 'God, have mercy on me, a sinner.'
>
> "I tell you that this man, rather than the other, went home justified before God. For all those who exalt themselves will be humbled, and those who humble themselves will be exalted."
>
> —LUKE 18:9–14

The Pharisee acted like someone devoted to God, but his motive revealed the intentions of his heart. His acts of faith supported his identity as someone elevated by God, someone superior to others. This religious leader's faith was merely a veneer for his own fears, weaknesses, and insecurities. By thanking God that he is "not like other people," the Pharisee comes dangerously close to elevating himself to be as righteous and holy as God. This is impossible for any human being, no matter how well intended, consistent, or good we think we are.

The prophet Isaiah expressed it this way: "All of us have become like one who is unclean, and all our righteous acts are like filthy rags; we all shrivel up like a leaf, and like the wind our sins sweep us away" (Isa. 64:6). The Hebrew phrase here translated as "filthy rags," *ukabeged ehdim*, literally refers to strips of cloth used by women during their monthly cycles.[2] It is a shocking, repugnant image—and that is exactly Isaiah's point! Our best gifts of service and heartfelt devotion can never come close to the pure and holy perfect righteousness of God.

When our self-righteousness becomes the source of our pride, we are just as self-reliant as any atheist. We work hard to appear like a good person and may even mistakenly believe that if we work hard enough, we can earn God's favor. But that is simply not possible! That is the very reason Jesus came to live on earth, die for our sins, rise again, and gift us with the Holy Spirit. Paul made this clear by referencing Psalm 14, along with Psalm 53 and Ecclesiastes 7, in his letter to the church at Rome: "There is no one righteous, not even one; there is no one who understands; there is no one who seeks God" (Rom. 3:10–11).

Christians are just as susceptible to pride as anyone else. The enemy knows how to adjust his strategy and play to our egos, inflating the way we see ourselves above others—and equal to God. It's the same ploy the devil used back in the Garden of Eden when he told Eve and Adam that they would not die if they ate the forbidden fruit—they would instead be like God (Gen. 3:5). The truth, however, is that we are not God and will never be His equal. We are His creation, made in His divine image, but not His equal.

We will never move from surviving to thriving unless we bow before Him as the Lord of all. God's Word clarifies our place before our Savior: "That at the name of Jesus every knee should bow, in heaven and on earth and under the earth, and every tongue acknowledge that Jesus Christ is Lord, to the glory of God the Father" (Phil. 2:10–11). Whether we're boastful in our own power, like Goliath, or self-righteous in our assessment of others, both lead right back to human pride and away from godly humility.

In order to thrive, only one source must anchor our identity, our power, and our worship.

HOLY HUMILITY

When we consider the kind of humility required to thrive, Jesus set the ultimate example. He accepted what God the Father considered necessary to restore relationship with human beings: incarnational reality, Word made flesh, God in the body of a baby in a manger in Bethlehem. He who was worthy of every accolade, title, luxury, and comfort went as low as He could go—no palace or golden cradle, no woven blankets and fur-lined crib, no attendants to see to His every need, no heralds to raise a royal banner and announce the news.

Instead, His early parents, a teenaged girl and an obedient carpenter, were forced to travel away from their home in order to comply with government requirements. Instead, they took shelter in a stable because there was no room in the inns because so many travelers had returned to their birthplace to be taxed. Instead, He was wrapped in cloths and laid in a feed trough lined with straw. Instead, awestruck shepherds came, along with foreigners bearing gifts. Instead, a star dazzled the night sky as angels heralded the news.

And that was only the beginning of Christ's ultimate journey in humility. He did not come from wealth and power, from religious leaders or educated scholars. He did not command an army or lead the religious order of His day. He did not oversee an army or seek political power or cultivate celebrity.

Instead Jesus waited until He was thirty years old and asked a ragtag band of scruffy fishermen and common laborers to join Him in His mission. Facing resistance from the establishment—the Roman government occupying Israel, the temple religious leaders waiting on a superhero Messiah to restore their nation to greatness, and the Jewish zealots anticipating a warrior to overthrow all oppression—Jesus refused to conform to anyone's expectations. He turned them all upside down and repeatedly and consistently demonstrated what it meant to surrender His own will to His Father's will. Instead of putting Himself first—He who is the only human to ever walk the earth and deserve its highest place of honor—put Himself last.

Jesus yielded Himself to God's perfect purposes in ways that we must emulate in order to grow and mature in our faith. Such a surrender of self seems counterintuitive and feels unnatural. Everything in our society, our culture, and our world tells us to compete, to compare, to fight, to win. We're taught to put ourselves first if we want to attain what we think we need and want. We're conditioned to make our lives the center of our universe around which everything and everyone else revolves.

> This is not the example set by Christ on the cross, though.

> This is not how we were meant to live.

> This is not what obedience to God looks like.

We are called to keep our egos surrendered to the power of God's Spirit within us. We are called to put ourselves last and others first. We are commanded to love our neighbors as ourselves. Consider the apostle Paul's admonition based on his explanation of the incredible example Jesus set for us:

> Do nothing out of selfish ambition or vain conceit. Rather, in humility value others above yourselves, not looking to your own interests but each of you to the interests of the others.
>
> In your relationships with one another, have the same mindset as Christ Jesus: Who, being in very nature God, did not consider equality with God something to be used to his own advantage; rather, he made himself nothing by taking the very nature of a servant, being made in human likeness. And being found in appearance as a man, he humbled himself by becoming obedient to death—even death on a cross!
>
> Therefore God exalted him to the highest place and gave him the name that is above every name, that at the name of Jesus every knee should bow, in heaven and on earth and under the earth, and every tongue acknowledge that Jesus Christ is Lord, to the glory of God the Father.
> —PHILIPPIANS 2:3–11

Jesus not only humbled Himself to be born in a manger, raised in a household of meager means, and doubted by the people He came to save. No, He maximized humility like no one before or after Him. Christ, the only perfect and innocent man, endured the ridicule, injustice, and torture of corrupt and selfish leaders. He who could have blinked and caused their death or summoned countless angels instead suffered brutality and anguish reserved only for the vilest of criminals.

Jesus sacrificed everything He was entitled to receive so that you and I would not receive what we deserved. He defeated death once and for all so that we may have eternal life. He showed us how to let go of the demands of our ego and instead yield to God's Spirit within us. We don't have to wait until an unexpected crisis or devastating loss to worship and obey God. Even if we didn't always respond in the faithful ways we wanted during the pandemic, we can always draw closer to Him. We can confess our pride and humble ourselves before the Lord, trusting in His healing power and cleansing love. We're told, "If my people who are called by my name humble themselves, and pray and seek my face and turn from their wicked ways, then I will hear from heaven and will forgive their sin and heal their land" (2 Chron. 7:14, ESV).

Holy humility opens up our hearts for God to work. His Word promises, "Humble yourselves before the Lord, and he will exalt you" (Jas. 4:10, ESV). Only when we stop relying on our own power can we exercise complete trust in God.

And when we exercise complete trust in God, we thrive!

TURN PRIDE INSIDE OUT

Holy humility always helps us find our way back home. Trusting in God and stepping out in faith, we discover the power, provision, and purpose to overcome any giant that stands before us and blocks our path. When scientific guidelines, state laws, and common sense made it clear that we must not convene in groups in order to defeat the virus, followers of Jesus trusted and obeyed. We knew that the church is not a building but the community of believers united by the bonds of God's love and the power of His Spirit.

As churches worldwide, including my own, were forced to move services online, we continued to worship together, pray together, learn together, and serve together. We are Christ's hands and feet, and even though we could not meet in person, shake hands, or give hugs, we recognized the need to be part of one body. We went online on our laptops, phones, and tablets and FaceTimed, Zoomed, and video-chatted with others. We used the time alone to draw closer to God and to seek Him and His wisdom. We humbled ourselves and experienced His presence.

The church not only survived but it thrived.

Consequently, one of the silver linings emerging from the pandemic has been people returning to God. It's the same phenomenon witnessed after the terrorist attacks of 9/11, or the devastation wrought by cataclysmic natural disasters such as tsunamis, hurricanes, tornadoes, earthquakes, and wildfires. When we experience painful losses so far beyond our control that they overwhelm us, we're forced to acknowledge our human limitations and seek God's power, protection, and purposes again. We regain perspective on what matters most to us and seek spiritual clarity and strength to get back on our feet again.

God wants us to continue to thrive. When we maintain holy humility by following Christ's example, we develop the faith to move mountains, to heal the sick, to free the prisoners, and to restore the broken. Fueled by God's power we experience the same kind of confidence David felt when facing Goliath. Rather than be intimidated by the boasts of a bully, be discouraged by the doubts of others, or succumb to the fear of the king, David fought his way—God's way. The shepherd boy anointed as king humbled himself before God and became exalted. David did what others deemed impossible!

David's faith declared a message as loud as anything said that day on the battlefield. "You say I'm too young, too inexperienced, too naïve, too unequipped, unprepared, and unaware? Then watch me! Watch what God is going to do through me. You say I can't, but God says I can. Don't think I can slay this giant? Watch me!"

When we trust in the Lord and rely on His power, then our humility sustains us with divine confidence. We turn our human pride inside out and experience the power of God. We may think "watch me!" would never be uttered by a humble servant of God, but I beg to differ.

What if "watch me" expresses the prophetic articulation of an individual who has been told, "You will never do it. You will never amount to anything. It is impossible to accomplish. Do not waste your time. You will never change. It can't be done, never in your wildest dreams!"

What if "watch me" might very well be the epitome of a grace-filled, Christ-centered, Spirit-led life?

I'm convinced "watch me" is not an expression of ego for those who follow Jesus. For believers, "watch me" is the expression of a person saved by grace. It's the neon arrow pointing to God's Spirit at work in me, through me, with me. It's a rallying cry for others to notice the miracle of your transformation from who you used to be without Christ to who you are becoming in Christ's likeness. The apostle Paul put it this way: "Imitate me, just as I also imitate Christ" (1 Cor. 11:1, NKJV).

Our desire is to emulate Paul's message so that we may all imitate Christ and become like Him: obedient to His heavenly Father, confident in His supernatural power, bold in the face of naysayers, and merciful beyond measure in displaying the love of God. Too often we're conditioned to focus on reasons why something can't be done rather than taking the next step toward providential possibility.

JUST WATCH ME!

We listen to authoritative voices—and these days I suspect everyone on social media thinks they're an authority—rather than to the Author and Finisher of our faith, Jesus Christ.

Rather than stare down the belittlement of bullies, the well-intentioned warnings of other warriors, and the frightening forecasts of frontline fearmongers, we must listen to God. He alone has the power to do what is impossible by our human standards. He alone is sovereign, all-mighty, all-powerful, all-knowing, all-loving. He alone chooses us to lead where others fear to tread.

It's time to redefine "watch me" as a battle cry for believers, an anthem of praise to the Source of our power, a song of rejoicing to celebrate what God has done for us, what He is doing right now, and what He is about to do. *"Watch me!"* The audacity; the forthrightness; the unbridled, uncompromised, outrageous declaration uttered by a person who has been saved by grace.

Watch me overcome that obstacle.

Watch me prove that the devil is a liar.

Watch me as I leave my family an inheritance of faith that will enable them to declare what the Lord has done for us.

Watch me as I go from glory to glory.

Watch me as I preach the Word in and out of season.

Watch me as I make disciples.

Watch me as I worship God in spirit and truth.

Watch me as I turn on the light and darkness flees.

Watch me overcome hate with love.

Watch me embody the idea that perfect love expels all fear.

Watch me demonstrate to the world that mercy triumphs over judgment.

Watch me exhibit love, joy, peace, patience, meekness, goodness, gentleness, temperance, mercy, and faith.

Watch me live like Jesus, love like Jesus, forgive like Jesus, and heal like Jesus.

I have full confidence that this is your season to slay your giant. This is your season, your hour, your moment to rise up and by faith in the name of Jesus, empowered by His precious Holy Spirit with unprecedented humility and grace, declare, *"Watch me!"*

Watch me overcome by the blood of the Lamb and the word of my testimony (Rev. 12:11).

Watch me conquer the mountain and possess the promise (1 Cor. 15:57).

Watch me live life abundantly (John 10:10).

Watch me arise and shine as the glory of God rises upon me (Isa. 60:1).

Watch me enlarge my territory, making room for what God is sending my way (Isa. 54:2).

Watch me trust and wait upon the Lord as my strength is renewed, as I mount up with wings as eagles, as I run without growing weary and walk without fainting (Isa. 40:31).

Watch me wait eagerly, along with all creation, for that

future day when God will reveal who His children really are (Rom. 8:19).

Watch me and be imitators of me as I am of Christ (1 Cor. 11:1).

Watch me as I walk in the way of the Lord, with the Word of the Lord, doing the will of the Lord.

Watch me as goodness and mercy, signs and wonders, healings and miracles, blessings and favor follow me all the days of my life.

Watch me exalt the name of Jesus every day, everywhere, through my actions words, deeds, thoughts, relationships, actions, interactions, and reactions without exception.

Watch me bring good news to the poor, freedom for the captives, healing to the brokenhearted, and declare the year of the Lord's favor.

Watch me take care of the widow and the orphan while simultaneously building a fire wall against the corruption of this world.

Watch me live, forgive, heal, bless, and change the world in the name of Jesus for the glory of Christ.

Watch me become nothing as Jesus is everything in me, with me, and through me!

Watch me live a holy, healed, healthy, happy, humble, hungry, honoring, hearty, and heroic life! And with that life, change the world!

If anyone doubts you, ridicules you, mocks you, taunts you, bullies you, denies you, or overlooks you, then you know what to say. If anyone doesn't like the way you look or the way you're dressed or your accent or the color of your skin or what you have and haven't done in the past, then you know how God wants you to respond. If you're too young or too old, if you're rich or poor, married or single, employed or unemployed, tall or short, big or little, then the answer remains the same. Turn your pride inside out, humble yourself before the Lord, and tell them: *"Watch me!"*

ALIVE TO THRIVE

Use the questions below to facilitate your reflection on what it looks like in your life to follow Christ's example of complete humility. Think of all areas in which you are trusting yourself, your good deeds, other people, or any sources other than God. Surrender them before Him in a time of prayer as you relinquish your pride, ego, and self-righteousness. The prayer below will get you started, but make it your own as you experience a fresh awareness of the Holy Spirit at work within you.

1. Where do you struggle the most with pride in your life? How has pride hindered your relationship with God in the past? How has it deterred your desire to be humble and focused on serving others?

2. How would you define humility based on what you've observed in other people? Now, how would

you define humility based on the example set by Jesus? What's the difference?

3. When have you experienced the kind of holy humility that fuels divine confidence in the power of the Lord? What are your "watch me!" experiences where others underestimated you or assumed you could not slay your giants?

Lord, I don't always feel as humble and fully confident as David did when he faced Goliath. I want to trust You, and You alone, as the source of my strength, security, and power. Abolish my pride, dear God, as I surrender my heart to You. Let Your Spirit fill me and lead me so that I can serve You by serving others, putting them before myself, just as Your Son did on the cross. Thank You for His sacrifice that paid the price for my sins. I praise You, Lord, for You are holy! Amen.

Chapter 7

HUNGRY FOR GOD—SATISFY YOUR CRAVING FOR MORE

*Our bodies need food to survive
just as our souls need spiritual food to thrive.*

*When we hunger for God, He nourishes us
with the bread of life and living water.*

I MISS MY FAVORITE *pastelitos*.

As a result of the pandemic and the requirement to shelter in place, many businesses closed, either temporarily or permanently, especially those deemed nonessential by government regulations. While some restaurants remained open for take-out orders, others closed their kitchens indefinitely. One such casualty was a favorite restaurant not far from where I live. An independent, family-owned establishment, the menu featured an eclectic assortment of Spanish, Mexican, Cuban, and Puerto Rican dishes. This place was a destination for many family special occasions—birthdays in particular—and visiting guests.

I never had a meal there I didn't enjoy. Each visit was a blessing for both body and spirit. If my enthusiasm sounds hyperbolic, I assure you I cannot say enough good things about the delicious, authentic cuisine and pleasant atmosphere of this restaurant. My kids used to tease me that I could do tableside commercials—and I probably would have if the owners had asked me, especially if they paid me with food!

Using family generational recipes along with their own experimental discoveries, the chefs cooking in the kitchen took great care with each dish, which was revealed in the authentic, homemade blend of flavors. My beloved *pastelitos*, basically little meat pies similar to empanadas, featured buttery, flaky crust on the outside and spicy, sausage-like filling on the inside. Sometimes I would also order crab *frituras*, deep-fried fritters stuffed with delicately seasoned crab meat. Completing my meal of items listed on the menu as appetizers was *asopao*, a rich, hearty gumbo-like soup brimming with bits of chicken, fish, seafood, or some combination.

For my entrée I usually couldn't resist *mofongo*—fried plantains mashed and seasoned with broth and spices—stuffed with churrasco steak, stewed chicken, or fried pork. Puerto Rican comfort food doesn't get any better than this! On special occasions, especially around Christmas and Easter, the restaurant offered *lechon asado*, an entire pig marinated in adobo (garlic, oregano, black pepper, vinegar, and water) before being slow-roasted over a bed of hot coals for many hours. Carved in thin slices and served with a side of *arroz y habichuelas*, or rice and beans, this was a meal fit for any king and his queen!

Then there's dessert, of course. Special occasions often provide license for indulgence—at least that was usually my excuse at this place. They always served a smooth coconut custard called *tembleque* as well as *arroz con dulce*, rice pudding with raisins and cinnamon. Around the holidays they also made *coquito*, similar to eggnog but made from coconut milk and various flavors such as chocolate, pistachio, or guava. Lingering over coffee or tea, we found the sweet end of our meals to be smooth and light, with always room for one last bite.

As much as I miss these savory dishes from my favorite eatery, I know that my loss is nothing compared to the losses experienced by millions of others. God was so gracious to provide an abundance of blessings for me and my family. As we sheltered at home, I was blessed with good food prepared by the loving hands of family members, and we never went without any essentials as many people experienced during times of quarantining at home. I continue to give God thanks and praise even as I seek to be a good steward of all He has entrusted to me in order to serve those in need.

So my purpose in sharing these happy culinary memories with you is not to lament my loss as much as to inspire you to consider your own favorite foods, meals, and locations. Whether it's your local pizzeria or pasta from a fine Italian restaurant, a beloved family member's made-from-scratch pies or croissants from the corner bakery, most of us can recall special flavors that make our mouths water. I suspect not being at liberty to enjoy those tasty treats whenever we wanted during our nation's shutdown also intensified our cravings. In fact, hunger is an odd physical sensation usually defined by an emptiness within—literally, within our stomachs.

But you only have to eat an entire bag of chips while binge-watching Netflix or scarf down a pint of Chunky Monkey at the end of a terrible day to know that eating for emotional comfort, not physical nourishment, is all too real. From infancy most people develop positive, pleasurable sensations around eating. Full bellies bring contentment. Empty stomachs cause distress. Hunger becomes a physical cue, often prompted by a variety of factors, that our bodies need fuel.

Our souls need fuel to survive as well. Some people find peace and solitude in nature, works of art, favorite pieces of music, or time spent with a close loved one. But in order to thrive, there's only one fuel source that nourishes, satisfies, empowers, and sustains us: relationship with the living God.

HOLY HUNGER

You only have to skip a few meals to understand hunger. Spiritual hunger, on the other hand, can be trickier to define. But the parallel to physical hunger gives us a good comparison to aid in our understanding.

In fact, the Bible is filled with comparisons that provide us with greater insight. One of the things I love about God's Word is the way it makes abstract concepts and ethereal matters accessible to us as human beings with intellectual, neurological, and psychological limitations. We cannot fully know the things of God because we are His creation. "'For my thoughts are not your thoughts, neither are your ways my ways,' declares the LORD. 'As the heavens are higher than the earth, so are my ways higher than your ways and my thoughts than your thoughts'" (Isa. 55:8–9). We are not on equal footing with Him; although as we've seen, our pride and the temptations of the enemy might lead us to such a false conclusion.

Despite our ultimate inability to fully grasp God's thoughts and ways, He still wants us to understand His truth. Therefore, throughout the Bible we see the use of comparison and contrast, of simile and metaphor to help us comprehend the divinely inspired meaning of things intangible. For example, throughout the Scriptures Jesus is variously described as the Lion of Judah, the Lamb of God, the Vine, the Good Shepherd, and the Bread of Life. These metaphoric monikers help us understand how He is fierce like a lion, sacrificial as a lamb, life-giving as a vine, vigilant and protective as a shepherd, and as essentially nourishing as bread.

This last metaphor, the Bread of Life, directly relates to the quality we must cultivate in order to grow closer to God and thrive: spiritual hunger. One might argue that this metaphor can be traced back to Genesis when Adam and Eve bit into the fruit God had forbidden them to eat. The fruit was from the tree of the knowledge of good and evil, which equates discernment of good and evil with consumption of its fruit (Gen. 2:16–18). Adam and Eve, tempted by the serpent, yielded to their hunger for rebellion, I suspect, more than for the fruit, which they nonetheless found pleasing to their eyes.

From there another symbolic instance of hunger occurred after the Israelites were delivered from slavery in Egypt. Curiously enough, they were in Egypt in the first place because of a terrible famine—the one Joseph, Jacob's favorite son, managed as Pharaoh's lieutenant after having been sold by his jealous brothers. As the Hebrew people began to outnumber the Egyptians, the natives felt threatened and enslaved the Jewish people, who had rebelled against God and disobeyed His commandments.

After the Israelites spent nearly four hundred years of captivity in a foreign land, God heard the prayers of His people and raised up Moses to lead them out of bondage and into the Promised Land. As you may recall, God even miraculously parted the Red Sea so that His people could escape, only to have the waters then come crashing down on the Egyptian soldiers in pursuit. This brief summary provides context for what happened next:

> In the desert the whole community grumbled against Moses and Aaron. The Israelites said to them, "If only we had died by the LORD's hand in Egypt! There we sat around pots of meat and ate all the food we wanted, but you have brought us out into this desert to starve this entire assembly to death."
>
> Then the LORD said to Moses, "I will rain down bread from heaven for you. The people are to go out each day and gather enough for that day. In this way I will test them and see whether they will follow my instructions.
> —EXODUS 16:2–4

This bread from heaven was called *manna,* a Hebrew word that literally means "What is it?" and reflects its unfamiliar origin.[1] More than the strange name, what is most striking here is God's gracious provision in the midst of such grumbling and ingratitude by the former captives He had just rescued. People are prone to short memories when it comes to God's goodness and generosity, and the Israelites were no exception. Not only did God provide bread for the children of Israel but water in the desert and meat from quail. He didn't send plagues and call Moses to lead them out of Egypt only to abandon them in the desert!

The Lord also used His provision to test His people's trust and reliance on Him. If they collected too much or not enough, they endured the consequences (Exod. 16:20). God only gave them enough for each day, except on the sixth day, when He provided enough for them to collect extra to have on hand for the next day, the Sabbath. As it turned out, God provided food and water for the Jewish people for decades as they wandered in the wilderness before allowing them to enter and claim the Promised Land.

Yet over all those years the Israelites still didn't get it.

They seemed to suffer from spiritual attention deficit disorder. Despite all that the Lord had done for them, they struggled to obey Him, trust Him, and keep His commandments—rules He had given them for their own benefit. They struggled to grasp how relationship with God nourished the hunger in their hearts just as the manna He provided nourished their bodies. Eventually they had to have this connection explained: "So He humbled you, allowed you to hunger, and fed you with manna which you did not know nor did your fathers know, that He might make you know that man shall not live by bread alone; but man lives by every word that proceeds from the mouth of the LORD" (Deut. 8:3, NKJV).

God made us to be more than physical bodies.

He gave us spirits that require connection to our life source, our Creator, our Father.

Without relying on God, we may survive for a while, but we will never thrive.

SOUL FOOD HAS NO SHELF LIFE

A significant aspect of hunger is the way it recurs regularly. Our bodies require nourishment and energy on a regular, ongoing basis. Just because you were hungry yesterday and ate a sumptuous meal that satisfied your appetite doesn't mean that you'll never hunger again. Your body digests the food you eat, transforms it into fuel for your body, eliminates what it does not need, and begins the cycle again. The marvel of our biological and physiological design yet again reflects the intricate brilliance of our Creator.

This repetitive cycle of hunger and satiation indeed seems intentional. When God provided manna for His people on their journey to the Promised Land, He gave them just enough for each day. When Jesus taught His followers how to pray, He instructed us to ask our Father to "give us this day our daily bread" (Matt. 6:11, NKJV). Christ Himself provided such a meal when He blessed the loaves and fishes from a boy's lunch and multiplied it into enough to feed more than five thousand people who came to hear His teaching (Matt. 14:13–21).

Most of us no longer hunt and gather our food each day. Our work provides for more than just our daily bread. In developed nations in our modern world, many of us have full kitchen cupboards, pantries, fridges, and freezers filled with food that's been preserved to extend its freshness. Some items such as dried beans, nuts, grains, and rice as well as canned goods are even considered to be "nonperishable" because they can be kept for months and years.

During the COVID-19 pandemic, many people stocked up because they feared stores and food producers might not have enough. Nonperishables were at a premium since no one knew how long the food supply might be interrupted. Unable to run to the store for desired ingredients or dine in our favorite restaurants, we made do with what we had on hand. Once again, many of us realized yet another luxury we had become accustomed to overlooking.

When we consider our spiritual hunger, we recognize that our souls require nourishment on a regular basis as well. No matter how often we pray, how many Bible passages we study and memorize, how frequently we attend church events or serve those in need, there's always room to grow closer to God. We could spend all day, every day praising and worshipping the Lord, and it would not be enough to fill our need for God's presence in our lives.

As eternal spiritual beings in temporal mortal bodies, we are designed to worship. Created in God's image, we long to be connected to the One who made us and knows us best just as children long to be connected to their parents. We want to belong and be part of something meaningful and significant, a cause that transcends our own ego, status, wealth, and fame. We want to fulfill the purpose for which God created us, giving ourselves in service so that others may experience His grace, mercy, peace, joy, and abundant blessings.

Seeking this kind of sustenance for our souls does not mean that our lives will be easy, comfortable, or free of suffering. On the contrary, the more aware we become of our desire to love, serve, and obey God, the more we often suffer the consequences of living in a fallen world of sinful people. In fact, Jesus included these people in His list of blessings that we usually call the Beatitudes, part of His Sermon on the Mount: "Blessed are those who hunger and thirst for righteousness, for they will be filled" (Matt. 5:6).

Rather than waiting, suffering, and trusting in the Lord, it's often tempting to take matters into our own hands when we're feeling empty inside. Instead of following Jesus and drawing close to God for soul food, we yield to temptation and seek instant gratification. I suspect so many of our emotional struggles result from our attempts to find spiritual nourishment in a worldly diet. We chase after goals, relationships, possessions, and achievements that we believe will make us happy and content, only to get them and discover the ache inside us remains. The prophet Isaiah expressed our spiritual longing, and our frustration when our own attempts to satisfy us fail, simply and poetically:

> Come, all you who are thirsty, come to the waters; and you who have no money, come, buy and eat! Come, buy wine and milk without money and without cost. Why spend money on what is not bread, and your labor on what does not satisfy? Listen, listen to me, and eat what is good, and you will delight in the richest of fare.
> —Isaiah 55:1–2

As the prophet points out, nothing we can purchase satisfies us the way God fills our hearts and nourishes our souls. This is the kind of meal that touches all our senses as we "delight in the richest of fare," knowing that God's goodness truly satisfies. It's the difference between gorging on the empty calories of junk food you barely taste and a multiple-course meal that fills your senses with exquisite smells, flavors, presentations, and textures.

When we rely on our own power, we strive merely to survive.

When we rely on God's power, we survive so we can thrive!

DEFAULT SETTINGS

Do you recall a series of candy bar commercials a few years ago that featured the tagline, "You're not yourself when you're hungry"? With different settings and characters the ads illustrated how snarling bullies and angry monsters transformed into sweet old ladies and docile neighbors once they bit into a Snickers bar. I believe we're not ourselves, not our true selves, when we settle for less than God's best. We remain frustrated, angry, self-serving people with insatiable appetites despite all we consume. As we are fed spiritual food and experience intimacy with God, we discover a depth of satisfaction nothing else can touch.

Nonetheless, we often resist obeying God's commandments, following His guidelines, and practicing the spiritual habits that deeply satisfy. We return instead to old addictions and destructive pleasures hoping to find what we're looking for only to grow frustrated when our empty attempts yield more disappointment, desperation, and discouragement. We go back to what we used to do before we encountered Jesus and invited His Spirit into our lives only to come up short. We look to our past efforts instead of God's future promises.

Perhaps there's no better illustration of this phenomenon than when Jesus' disciples went fishing one night not long after their Master had risen from the dead:

> Afterward Jesus appeared again to his disciples, by the Sea of Galilee. It happened this way: Simon Peter, Thomas (also known as Didymus), Nathanael from Cana in Galilee, the sons of Zebedee, and two other disciples were together. "I'm going out to fish," Simon Peter told them, and they said, "We'll go with you." So they went out and got into the boat, but that night they caught nothing.
>
> Early in the morning, Jesus stood on the shore, but the disciples did not realize that it was Jesus.

He called out to them, "Friends, haven't you any fish?"
"No," they answered.

He said, "Throw your net on the right side of the boat and you will find some." When they did, they were unable to haul the net in because of the large number of fish.

Then the disciple whom Jesus loved said to Peter, "It is the Lord!" As soon as Simon Peter heard him say, "It is the Lord," he wrapped his outer garment around him (for he had taken it off) and jumped into the water. The other disciples followed in the boat, towing the net full of fish, for they were not far from shore, about a hundred yards. When they landed, they saw a fire of burning coals there with fish on it, and some bread.

Jesus said to them, "Bring some of the fish you have just caught." So Simon Peter climbed back into the boat and dragged the net ashore. It was full of large fish, 153, but even with so many the net was not torn.

—John 21:1–11

I find it interesting but not surprising that after Jesus had been crucified, buried, and resurrected, His disciples resumed doing what they knew best: fishing. It probably comforted them to return to their boats and nets and do something so familiar they didn't even have to think about it. There was only one problem—they were no longer who they used to be! Instead of experiencing the fullness of the risen Savior, the excitement of being new creatures in Christ, they reverted to their default settings.

We all have default settings, even if that's not the term we use. On your smartphone, laptop, and the computer in your vehicle, as well as many appliances and systems in your home now, you have the original programmed operational sets known as default settings. If a malicious virus attacks or something in a system goes wrong, you can always reset the device to go back to default settings. They're basic, familiar, and have been around since the system was created.

The disciples went back to doing what they were doing before they met Jesus. They returned to their default settings. And what were the results? They caught nothing!

You don't have to be a computer whiz to realize that when they returned to their default settings, they ended up with a big fat zero. They experienced what happens when you go back to your old lifestyle, back to how you lived prior to knowing Christ: *you catch nothing.* Why? It's very simple: there's nothing back there!

> There's nothing when you go back.
>
> There's nothing when you look back.
>
> There's nothing when you think back.
>
> There's nothing when you speak back.
>
> There's nothing when you text back.
>
> There's nothing when you search back.
>
> There's nothing when you google back.
>
> There's nothing in your past.

There's nothing of any significant value when you go back to what you were doing before you met Jesus. There's nothing in the past behavior, there's nothing in that previous relationship, there's nothing at your former job.

> There's nothing in the old way of thinking.
>
> If God took you out, why would you want to go back?

If you want your hunger to help you thrive in the power of the living God, then it's time to change your default setting to Jesus! Don't go back to the sinful routines and old messages in your mind. Don't return to a diet of worldly pleasures and empty possessions. *Change your default settings!*

Forget what happened all those years ago! Don't even think about what you used to do. The Bible warns us clearly, "Forget the former things; do not dwell on the past" (Isa. 43:18). Simply stated, don't go there.

Don't think there.

Don't speak there.

Don't live there.

There's nothing there!

When you make a final determination that you will never look back, think back, or speak back, then God's glorious future for you opens up! Your hunger is filled with joy, peace, hope, purpose, and unconditional love. Don't eat what has long since expired and is no longer palatable or nourishing! You'll get sick or even contract food poisoning.

If you want to thrive at the Lord's table of bounty, then make this declaration: I am not going back. Say it out loud and mean it: I am not going back to my default settings.

I am not going back to overspending.

I am not going back to addiction.

I am not going back to being a victim.

I am not going back to perpetual brokenness.

I am not going back to destructive criticism.

I am not going back to past failures.

I am not going back to that abusive relationship.

I am not going back to the old me.

I am not going back!

My friend, you never have to go back, because God has your back! His Word promises, "Then your salvation will come like the dawn, and your wounds will quickly heal. Your godliness will lead you forward, and the glory of the Lord will protect you from behind" (Isa. 58:8, NLT).

Default settings may have allowed you to survive, but they will never help you thrive!

FROM LONGING TO LEGACY

This scene with Jesus and the disciples on the shore actually parallels His first encounter with several of them, one with similar results:

> He got into one of the boats, the one belonging to Simon, and asked him to put out a little from shore. Then he sat down and taught the people from the boat. When he had finished speaking, he said to Simon, "Put out into deep water, and let down the nets for a catch."
> Simon answered, "Master, we've worked hard all night and haven't caught anything. But because you say so, I will let down the nets."
> When they had done so, they caught such a large number of fish that their nets began to break.
> —LUKE 5:3–6

We can draw a number of applicable truths here on how to find food for our souls. First, to catch fish, the disciples had nets. As experienced fishermen, they knew that you need something to catch something. Some people would like to catch fish without a net, without bait, or without a rod, but you need to be ready in order to receive what God has for you. Too often you're asking God for fish and He's asking you, "Where's your net?"

If you want to thrive, stop asking for things that you don't have the ability to manage. You need a net before you get the fish. You need to get in touch with your spiritual hunger before you digest what God will give you. Before you master it, you must learn to manage it!

Why? Because the Bible says that we must do our part before we can receive God's part.

You need faith to move mountains.

You need holiness to see God.

You need courage to speak truth.

You need truth to set you free.

You need to confess Jesus to be saved.

You need the blood of the Lamb to overcome.

You need to pray for God's will to be done.

You need love to change the world.

You need something to catch something!

The practices that will allow you to receive soul satisfaction from God require activation. With most food, you need to prepare and cook it before eating it. With soul food, you must prepare as well. How?

Faith is a net.

Praise is a net.

Worship is a net.

The Word of God is a net.

The name of Jesus is a net.

Living right is a net.

God provides more when you can manage more. If you're not aware of your soul's true hunger, then you won't know how to enjoy the divine nourishment of His Spirit. We're told, "The one who manages the little he has been given with faithfulness and integrity will be promoted and trusted with greater responsibilities. But those who cheat with the little they have been given will not be considered trustworthy to receive more" (Luke 16:10, TPT). If you're not managing the kitchen you do have, then why would God want to give you more food? You must be a steward of your blessings in order to be entrusted with greater blessings.

Once again we see the way our physical hunger and spiritual hunger overlap: "If you have not handled the riches of this world with integrity, why should you be trusted with the eternal treasures of the spiritual world? And if you've not been proven faithful with what belongs to another, why should you be given wealth of your own?" (Luke 16:11–12, TPT). As you grow and mature in your faith, you advance from management to mastery.

Your longing becomes your legacy!

YOUR NET WORTH

When you return the nourishment God gives you by serving Him, then He multiplies it. Jesus instructed His disciples to cast their nets again as people changed by the power of God's grace, rewarding them with His own example as a servant leader: "When they landed, they saw a fire of burning coals there with fish on it, and some bread. Jesus said to them, 'Bring some of the fish you have just caught'" (John 21:9–10). He combined what He had with what they gave Him to produce a meal to be shared. But He also demonstrated that the gift was in the fellowship, not the quantity of fish caught or cooked on the beach. God wants His people to hunger for Him and His will more than the blessings He provides. He wants us to have the kind of intense longing of the psalmist: "As the deer pants for streams of water, so my soul pants for you, my God" (Ps. 42:1).

Do you love Him more than what He provides for you?

Do you love the miracle or the Miracle Worker?

Do you love the Blesser or just His blessings?

If you want to experience deep satisfaction for the holy hunger within your soul, then give God what He gave to you. He whispers to our hearts, *I give you eternal life; now give Me back your life so I can use your life to glorify and magnify My name.* "Give generously and generous gifts will be given back to you, shaken down to make room for more. Abundant gifts will pour out upon you with such an overflowing measure that it will run over the top! Your measurement of generosity becomes the measurement of your return" (Luke 6:38, TPT).

When your gift is combined with His grace, then God will receive all of the glory!

Even when we stumble and fall, our Lord continues to

forgive us, bless us, and feed us. Returning to our fishermen on the beach with Jesus, you can't help but notice the very specific number of fish caught: "So Simon Peter climbed back into the boat and dragged the net ashore. It was full of large fish, 153, but even with so many the net was not torn" (John 21:11). Now you probably know that nothing in the Bible is there accidentally or by coincidence, and neither is our net filled with 153 fish. Why this exact number?

To solve this mystery we must remember who's in the spotlight with Jesus here: Simon Peter. The same Peter who promised that he would never abandon his Master despite Jesus' prophetic utterance: "I tell you the truth, Peter—this very night, before the rooster crows, you will deny three times that you even know me" (Matt. 26:34, NLT).

So here Peter's catch is 153.

This total is fifty times more than the three denials, which totals one hundred fifty (3 x 50 = 150), even with the three denials added (150 + 3 = 153). If my math seems confusing or far-fetched, then let me make my point clear: God will always provide a greater return than you give Him. Living in Christ, your good days will be greater than your bad days.

> Your blessings will outnumber your blunders.

> Your victories will exceed your defeats.

> Your days of joy will exponentially be greater than your days of sorrow.

> Your life of holiness will be infinitely greater than your season of sinfulness.

When you are nourished by the bread of life and your thirst is quenched by living water, your strength will never fail. As you thrive, your new net will catch more fish but will not break! "It was full of large fish, 153, but even with so many the net was not torn" (John 21:11). You only have to compare this to that first scene when Jesus called these fishermen to join Him to see the difference: "And this time their nets were so full of fish they began to tear!" (Luke 5:6, NLT).

Three and a half years prior, the same people in the same place followed the same instructions, and their net broke. Now the scene replayed itself with a crucial difference: their net did not break. Same process, different outcome. Because of Christ's sacrifice on the cross and His resurrection, our strength is not based on what we do but on what He did! Jesus defeated death, and the devil himself can never steal your strength, your joy, your anointing, and your promise.

Christ created a way by which the strength stems not from an external action but rather by an internal truth. In other words, He placed the source of your strength not in your muscles, not in your eyes, not in your mouths, not in what you eat, but in a place the devil can never touch—the Spirit of God inside of you. You can do everything through Him who gives you strength (Phil. 4:13). No matter how weak and hungry you may feel at times, God will provide strength and power.

No wonder then that on the night before He was betrayed and led to His death, Jesus gathered with His disciples for a Passover meal. There He took the bread and the wine on the table and transformed them into eternal, living symbols of the sacrifice He made for us all:

> While they were eating, Jesus took bread, and when he had given thanks, he broke it and gave it to his disciples, saying, "Take and eat; this is my body."
>
> Then he took a cup, and when he had given thanks, he gave it to them, saying, "Drink from it, all of you. This is

my blood of the covenant, which is poured out for many
for the forgiveness of sins."

—MATTHEW 26:26–28

Nourished by the body and blood of Jesus Christ, our Lord
and Savior, we shall be filled with His Spirit and empowered
to change the world. Let your holy hunger fuel your journey.

Our strength is Jesus!

Our strength is Christ and Christ alone.

This is why we can say, "Greater is He that is in me than
He that is in the world!" (See 1 John 4:4.)

When you are entrusted with more, your net will not break—
because this net has been sewn by the nail-pierced hands of
Jesus.

Your faith net will not break.

Your family net will not break.

Your future net will not break.

Your holiness net will not break.

Your love net will not break.

Your peace net will not break.

Your favor net will not break.

Your health net will not break.

Your financial net will not break.

The net of your children and your children's children
will not break.

Your net worth is priceless!

Hunger for God and you shall always be filled with His Spirit!

ALIVE TO THRIVE

The questions below are designed to help you reflect on your spiritual hunger and the ways God nourishes the longings of your heart. Similarly, the prayer below will help you begin sharing your heart with the Lord as you draw closer to Him, discovering the fulfillment only His Spirit can bring.

1. When have you experienced a hunger for God? How did He provide nourishment for you during those times?

2. What are your default settings—the habits, patterns, and old ways you slip back into when you're struggling, stressed, or only surviving?

3. How can you draw strength from the power of Christ as you develop new practices and spiritual disciplines? Which spiritual practices—praying, reading your Bible, praising, worshipping, and singing hymns, just to name a few—provide nourishment for your soul?

Jesus, thank You for the sacrifice You made so that I could experience new life. May I look to Your example as I seek to abandon my old default settings and cast new nets according to Your leading. Give me strength to resist temptation for anything other than the living water and bread of life You offer. Amen.

Chapter 8

HONORING OR HONORARY— DEDICATE YOUR DILIGENCE

In order to thrive, we must honor God in our thoughts, our words, and our deeds.

Honor requires us to align the attitudes of our hearts with the actions of our lives.

ONE OF THE unexpected blessings of sheltering at home during the pandemic was quality time with family. I confess that I consider multitasking a spiritual gift and have had to be intentional about resting, relaxing, and recreating. My wife has told me that she believes God commanded us to keep the Sabbath as a day of rest with me in mind. After all, the Lord Himself modeled the practice even though He does not need rest, not the way you and I need it: "By the seventh day God had finished the work he had been doing; so on the seventh day he rested from all his work" (Gen. 2:2).

Although I was actually busier while quarantining at home than ever before (I joked that I must have been lazy before by comparison), I also enjoyed time, especially in the evenings, with just my wife, Eva, and a handful of other family members. We actually don't feel like grandparents—at least not the stereotypical, gray-haired kind—in retirement, but we now have two grandchildren who bring so much joy to our lives. Their innocence, curiosity, and sense of excitement are inherently contagious.

One of the prerogatives of a grandfather, in my humble opinion, is to introduce his grandchildren to all his favorites and indoctrinate them at an early age. From favorite sports teams to ice cream flavors, Disney characters to holiday traditions, I love sharing things I love with these little ones. If you know anything about me, then you won't be shocked to know that I start them watching the original *Star Trek* series at an early age, selectively curated of course so there's nothing too scary. From there, as they grow older, I plan to move on to *Next Generation*, the feature films with original characters, and various spinoffs.

There's a method to my madness, because I also get to share another related passion with my grandkids: stargazing. Now, I've always been a math and science geek and would probably be working in the engineering field if God hadn't called me to serve as a pastor, which partially explains why I'm a lifelong Christ-following, Spirit-filled Trekkie—and why I say that I preach like William Shatner's Captain Kirk but think like Leonard Nimoy's Mr. Spock!

Fueled by my love of space, a couple of years ago we bought a telescope and set it up on our back patio. Getting the telescope focused and then navigating the seasonal night skies requires patience. It forces me to slow down and focus on the present moment. Looking for Jupiter and its moons sometimes feels like looking for the proverbial needle in a sky full of needles. But then suddenly there it is! The reality of seeing its red spot and coppery brown appearance is better than any CGI special effects.

My grandkids enjoy seeing various stars and planets, but I suspect they also like seeing me get so excited about our heavenly discoveries. And I can't resist the organic opportunities that occur to share about the Creator of those celestial bodies:

"Lift up your eyes and look to the heavens: Who created all these? He who brings out the starry host one by one and calls forth each of them by name. Because of his great power and mighty strength, not one of them is missing" (Isa. 40:26). Out of all the things I want to share with my grandchildren, knowing God and honoring Him takes priority.

When we appreciate something as magnificent as these twinkling, glimmering shapes coming into focus, knowing they are millions of light-years away, the experience is humbling, inspiring, and awe-filling all at once. The beauty of God's creation reflects His majesty, holiness, and goodness. There's no response except to praise and worship the One who made them all. And there's no doubt. As if answering Isaiah's question of "Who created all these?" we find an explicit answer in Amos: "He who made the Pleiades and Orion, who turns midnight into dawn and darkens day into night, who calls for the waters of the sea and pours them out over the face of the land—the LORD is his name" (Amos 5:8).

Like an author signing her painting or a sculptor chiseling his name at the base of a statue, God deserves all the credit for being the divine artist He is. Rather than worshipping God's creation in any of its forms, we turn to the Creator as our focus. If we want to thrive, then we learn that honoring God means seeing His fingerprints wherever we are.

Honor is how we show that our beliefs and actions are aligned.

LOOK UP

Gazing up at the stars, comets, planets, and galaxies, I feel as if I'm honoring God by admiring and appreciating the brilliant intricacies of His creation. I've long believed that science doesn't oppose God's presence in the architecture of all things but instead affirms it. Nonetheless, I'm careful to give the Lord all the credit, glory, and honor for everything in creation, mindful of His warning to the people of Israel after they left Egypt:

> Therefore watch yourselves very carefully, so that you do not become corrupt and make for yourselves an idol, an image of any shape, whether formed like a man or a woman, or like any animal on earth or any bird that flies in the air, or like any creature that moves along the ground or any fish in the waters below. And when you look up to the sky and see the sun, the moon and the stars—all the heavenly array—do not be enticed into bowing down to them and worshiping things the LORD your God has apportioned to all the nations under heaven....
>
> Be careful not to forget the covenant of the LORD your God that he made with you; do not make for yourselves an idol in the form of anything the LORD your God has forbidden. For the LORD your God is a consuming fire, a jealous God.
>
> —DEUTERONOMY 4:15–19, 23–24

Maybe you assume this passage isn't as relevant to you and me today as it was to the Israelites thousands of years ago. Such a conclusion would be mistaken, however, because the temptation to practice idolatry remains as strong as ever in human nature. We may not be tempted to form a golden calf and worship it like the children of Israel did in the desert, but we still confront the urge to make gold our god, whether literally or figuratively. Every time we allow greed, envy, and comparison to fuel our pursuit of money in order to buy more, borrow more, BMW more, bling more, be more, we're chasing idols. Every time we define ourselves by status symbols and bank balances rather than the truth of our identity in Christ, we're bowing before other gods.

Some people are uncomfortable with the fact that the Lord our God is a jealous God, especially when His jealousy is described as a "consuming fire"; it conjures up ideas of human jealousy gone to extremes. We think of exes shaming us on social media or stalkers showing up at our doors. But I think it's a good thing to remember God's jealousy. Why? Because it underscores His passionate pursuit of us, His eternal love for us, and His priceless sacrifice on the cross. There was only one thing powerful enough to motivate God's willingness to allow His beloved Son to come to earth in the form of a human being; face persecution and humiliation; and die a slow, excruciating death filled with torturous pain: *love.*

We tend to use it so often that its familiarity dilutes the unfathomable potency of its message, but John 3:16 distills the essence of the gospel so efficiently: "For God so loved the world that He gave His only begotten Son, that whoever believes in Him should not perish but have everlasting life" (NKJV). God made us with the freedom to choose whether we would love Him in return, and we experience the fullness of His love despite our sinful rebellion. We didn't deserve the gift of grace Jesus paid at Calvary. "But God demonstrates his own love for us in this: While we were still sinners, Christ died for us" (Rom. 5:8).

Considering such illogical, irrational, irreversible, perfect love, there's only one way to show our gratitude—honoring Him with the gift of our lives.

YES, YOUR HONOR

Honor is a concept that I fear has lost some of its power in our modern language. This is partly because its meaning is by definition general and abstract rather than specific and concrete. What demonstrates honor and provides evidence, though, is very tangible and discernable to our senses. Because honoring God is best understood as a practice, an active lifestyle exercising honor, rather than as a concept. It's walking the talk and putting our faith in action and our money where our ministry is.

Throughout the Bible honor stands as a pillar of foundational strength, commitment, and devotion to our faith in God. He alone is worthy of the highest respect, adoration, and esteem we can offer: "You are worthy, our Lord and God, to receive glory and honor and power, for you created all things, and by your will they were created and have their being" (Rev. 4:11). This is the posture of our hearts in our relationship to Him, not merely a one-time offering or occasional acknowledgment.

In other words, you can't honor God by only going to church once a week or saying a prayer before meals. Your life and lifestyle are intertwined just as your beliefs and practice of those beliefs go hand-in-hand. Honoring God reveals itself in every detail of your day. Do you seek to put Him first? Do you follow the Spirit's guidance or the pull of your sensual appetites? Do you honor God with your thoughts?

Do you honor Him with your words?

Do you honor Him at home?

Do you honor Him at work?

Do you honor Him when you're alone?

Do you honor Him when you're in a crowd?

Do you honor Him with your body?

Do you honor Him in your relationships?

Do you honor Him in your marriage?

Do you honor Him in your family?

In addition to honoring God first, we are commanded in the Bible to honor certain people, including our fathers and mothers (Exod. 20:12), elders (Lev. 19:32) and rulers (1 Pet. 2:17), church leaders (1 Tim. 5:17), and others who faithfully serve Jesus (Phil. 2:29). God also instructs us to honor certain divinely ordained institutions, including marriage (Heb. 13:4) and Sabbath rest (Exod. 20:8–11). Honoring these through godly obedience goes beyond cultural, social, and historical customs and trends. The Lord established these relationships and institutions for His purposes, and their significance remains eternal. We honor these by obeying God's instructions and valuing them as He values them, nothing more and nothing less.

When the word *honor* appears in our English translation of these scriptures, it's most often from the Hebrew *b'khavod*, which carries a sense of something heavy, something deep within your body and organs; a visceral sense of respect and appreciation. Within the original language, *honor* covers a spectrum of meanings with a range of nuanced differences. Overall, though, it carries a sense of how much you think something is worth—its quality, its value. It can reflect a shared sense of values or recognize different perspectives that are highly regarded. Honor can also express something earned as well as something given.

Consider it this way. I have been blessed to receive honorary doctorates from Northwest, William Jessup, and Baptist University of the Américas. These educational institutions awarded me this honorary degree to recognize my ministry, my passion for Christ, and my relationships in their communities. They did not award those doctorates because I completed coursework, passed comprehensive exams, and then wrote and defended a book-length dissertation, which is the usual route to attaining a doctorate in most of the liberal arts.

By conferring an honorary degree, the universities made a noteworthy gesture of acknowledgment. While I'm grateful for their recognition, I nonetheless respect the distinction between their *honorary* gifts and the degrees *honoring* the work I did in fulfilling established requirements, such as my undergraduate degree and master's.

God deserves our honor as more than just a special acknowledgment or token gesture. His lovingkindness, grace, mercy, and blessings extend to our past, our present, and our future. There's no way we can ever repay the Lord for all He's done for us. At best we can only do what He's created us to do, fulfilling our purpose for His kingdom out of love, devotion, and gratitude. This is the secret to thriving in its simplest, purest form. When we do what God designed us to do, then we experience the peace, passion, and purpose that brings true contentment.

It won't be easy, though. No matter how much we desire to honor Him by becoming a living sacrifice, we almost always encounter obstacles along the way. The silver lining, though, is that every obstacle only sends us back to God, relying on His Spirit for the power to overcome.

LOVE AND HONOR

When we honor God with our lives, we also honor what He values most. And what does God honor most? People! How do I know this? Because Jesus made it very clear in His response to a different version of this same question:

"Teacher, which is the greatest commandment in the Law?"
Jesus replied: "'Love the Lord your God with all your heart and with all your soul and with all your mind.' This

is the first and greatest commandment. And the second
is like it: 'Love your neighbor as yourself.' All the Law and
the Prophets hang on these two commandments."
                                    —MATTHEW 22:36–40

Loving God and loving our neighbors are intertwined. If we
love God, then we will automatically seek to serve and love
our neighbors. This reflects the way honor extends beyond our
direct relationship with God and encompasses other people.
In fact, the concept of honor in God's Word usually includes a
sense of community, groups of others, both personal (such as
family and friends) and public (such as acquaintances, authorities, and government officials).

In the pages of Scripture we see that honor was something
given by others within our community and often reflected on
an individual's family, tribe, and nation. Honor and shame carried great weight in the ancient world during the time Jesus
lived on the earth. Showing public honor to a person revealed
their good deeds to everyone, while shame cast a stain of association extending far beyond the offender. For example, in the
New Testament we see how Gamaliel was "held in honor by
all the people" (Acts 5:34, ESV), while in the Old we notice
that Mordecai was honored publicly, which also cast shame on
Haman (Esther 6).

Proverbs often contrasts honor and shame, often pairing
them with wisdom and folly to show how they're causally
related: "The wise inherit honor, but fools get only shame"
(Prov. 3:35). We're also cautioned not to cheapen honor by
awarding it to those who are undeserving: "Like snow in
summer or rain in harvest, honor is not fitting for a fool" (Prov.
26:1). Similarly, overlooking someone or something deserving
of honor, whether intentional or not, would be a mistake.

In fact, God's Word often urges us to honor those whom
others shun, ignore, or reject. This reflects the example that

Jesus set for us. Christ disregarded the cultural, social, and even religious customs of tradition and never hesitated to love, heal, and forgive the sinners, outcasts, and rejects of society. He mingled with tax collectors, fishermen, and prostitutes, those the Jewish religious establishment considered unclean and unworthy of their notice. When the Pharisees asked Jesus why He included these undesirables, He said, "It is not the healthy who need a doctor, but the sick. I have not come to call the righteous, but sinners to repentance" (Luke 5:31–32).

Christ came to serve those in need and to save the lost. He ignored class structure and bias based on gender, ethnicity, religion, age, education, economic status, and social standing. Jesus addressed the hearts of people willing to drop their pretenses and defenses and reminded us that we are to focus on our own sins and not those of others. God's Word reinforces Jesus' example plainly and directly:

> My brothers and sisters, believers in our glorious Lord Jesus Christ must not show favoritism. Suppose a man comes into your meeting wearing a gold ring and fine clothes, and a poor man in filthy old clothes also comes in. If you show special attention to the man wearing fine clothes and say, "Here's a good seat for you," but say to the poor man, "You stand there" or "Sit on the floor by my feet," have you not discriminated among yourselves and become judges with evil thoughts?
>
> —James 2:1–4

Favoritism, racism, bias, and discrimination not only dishonor other people but they dishonor God. Each one of us is His child created in His divine image while being uniquely made for distinct purposes. The Bible tells us, "We all have different gifts, according to the grace given to each of us." (Rom. 12:6). We can help everyone thrive when we honor what God has placed in each person.

SACRIFICE AND STEWARDSHIP

Honor takes the high road and, like love, is not boastful, proud, arrogant, selfish, greedy, or spiteful. Honor sees the goodness of God and draws others' attention to it. Honor plays fair and calls out the best in everyone. Cheating and winning at any cost erodes and tarnishes any sense of attainment. As the apostle Paul wrote to his protégé Timothy, "An athlete is not crowned unless he competes according to the rules" (2 Tim. 2:5, ESV). There is never honor, not the kind that reflects the character of Christ and the Word of God, in doing whatever it takes to beat others.

Honor also maintains a lifestyle that reflects God's glory, grace, goodness, and generosity. "Do you not know that your bodies are temples of the Holy Spirit, who is in you, whom you have received from God?" (1 Cor. 6:19). How we act, which habits we keep, and what we do all reflect the extent to which we honor God in our lives. When we resist sexual immorality, we control our bodies "in holiness and honor" to please our Lord (1 Thess. 4:3–4, ESV). When we have no restraints or self-discipline, we yield to "dishonorable passions," as Paul describes them (Rom. 1:26, ESV).

Honoring our bodies as homes for God's Spirit means more than abstaining from immorality; it means we serve as responsible stewards of the precious gift of life we've been given. We should all respect our physical bodies by doing what we know promotes good health and prevents injury and disease. Self-care that is not selfish, sinful, and indulgent honors God. We show our gratitude and appreciation to our Creator by taking good care of our physical, mental, emotional, and psychological needs. We eat healthy food and get enough rest; we exercise and give up destructive, addictive habits undermining our overall health.

Beyond our bodies, we're also called to be good stewards

who honor His glorious natural creation. God first made Adam and Eve in charge of the plants and animals in the Garden of Eden, but even after they disobeyed Him and left, God still held them responsible for taking care of His creation. Our glorious planet perhaps now more than ever is in need of honoring. We're called to take care of God's land, His waters, His air, His vast and dazzling array of living creatures. He holds us accountable for stewarding our earth's resources and environmental systems.

Sometimes when I'm looking through my telescope and gazing at the moon's surface or the Big Dipper, I'm reminded that God wants us to be good stewards of our intellects, imaginations, and creativity. We honor Him with the art we create, the stories we tell, and the music we compose. We honor Him by utilizing our unique gifts, talents, abilities, and experiences and boldly going where no one else has gone before!

THE SECRET TO THRIVING

If we want to thrive, not merely to survive the trials and turmoil of the pandemic, economic uncertainty, and social unrest, then we must honor God in all that we do. We have to stop allowing our worry, fear, anxiety, depression, and shame to steal the joy, peace, power, and purpose God gives us. One of the ways we defend against these powerful, debilitating emotions is by practicing habits that honor God. No matter what you do, do it unto the Lord!

> If you're tired of all the political gridlock and divisiveness, then honor God with your life.

> If you're tired of others lying, cheating, hurting, deceiving, and exploiting, then honor God with your life.

If you're tired of being afraid of the next crisis, disaster, catastrophe, or calamity, then honor God with your life.

If you're tired of feeling lonely, disconnected, isolated, and cut off, then honor God with your life.

If you're sick and tired of being sick and tired, then honor God with your life.

And how do you honor Him each day of your life? By claiming His promises each morning when you wake up. By refusing to listen to the lies of the devil. By residing in the power of the Holy Spirit. By obeying His Word and spending time alone with Him. By praising His holy name and worshipping Him for who He is.

I wrote this book because during the pandemic and all that's happened in the recent past, so many people came to me worried, afraid, depressed, angry, anxious, desperate, and sometimes hopeless. They wanted me to reassure them with what I know to be true. They wanted to hear what I was doing to combat all the stress, negativity, and criticism tearing people apart. They wanted to know my secret for trusting God through unprecedented, unparalleled, and unexpected events. And do you know what I told them?

I told them the short version of everything I'm sharing with you in this book!

Long before any of us ever heard of COVID-19 or the social and economic upheaval that continues to unfold around us, I made a commitment to honor God with the life He has given me. Many years ago I decided that the key was to declare God's truth over each day before I ever get out of bed in the morning. I determined that I was going to do everything in my power to make sure my life's work, every minute of every day, adhered to God's will and His Spirit's direction. I chose to honor God by embracing the abundant life of blessings He offers me.

And my shorthand for this commitment to honor God in all that I do was the word *thrive*. I like this word because it succinctly expresses what it means to live a Christ-centered, God-honoring, Spirit-filled life. A life that is holy, healed, healthy, happy, humble, hungry, and honoring!

I am no different than you when it comes to thriving. Each of us has different gifts but the same Giver, different tasks but the same Master, different challenges but the same Spirit empowering us to overcome every giant, every obstacle, every hindrance that gets in our way. If you want to thrive, then it's time to shout to the Lord, "Thy kingdom come! Thy will be done! On earth as it is in heaven!"

Thriving is about restoring order from chaos, dancing instead of mourning, and receiving beauty for ashes. It's about building arks, chasing rainbows, parting seas, claiming the Promised Land, and slaying giants. It's about refusing to give up when others tell you something cannot be done. It's about trusting God and stepping out in faith. About believing that the battle belongs to the Lord. About knowing who you are and whose you are. About following Jesus and believing beyond any shadow of a doubt that nothing can separate you from His perfect love.

Thriving is about ending the pursuit of perfection and embracing all that God says is perfect in your life. It's about no longer relying on your own efforts and resisting the temptation to do things like others do them. It's about throwing off the armor that doesn't belong to you and doesn't fit. It's about remembering where you've come from and what you've overcome to get there. It's about learning from every bear and lion, every stumble and stall along the way. It's about getting up again and asking God to give you strength for the next step and the next one. It's about choosing your weapons carefully and asking God to guide your slingshot and to direct your fishing net.

Thriving is about *honoring.*

Honoring is about *obedience.*

STOP STRIVING; START THRIVING

If you want to thrive, my friend, then you must stop whatever dishonors God in your life and continue doing everything that honors Him. We're told, "As obedient children, do not be conformed to the passions of your former ignorance, but as he who called you is holy, you also be holy in all your conduct, since it is written, 'You shall be holy, for I am holy'" (1 Pet. 1:14–16, ESV). Holiness is impossible by our own efforts and power. Holiness is not about striving but about thriving in the power of the Holy Spirit! When we are led by the Spirit, we tap into supernatural resources beyond our ability to measure or comprehend.

Honoring God by what you do empowers you to defeat the enemy and claim the victory for the holy kingdom. So many people say they want to thrive but refuse to submit in full obedience to the Lord. They want something they're not willing to pay for with their lives. As the old saying goes, grace is free but it ain't cheap! The priceless gift of salvation can never be repaid, but we can honor the one who gave it by devoting our lives to Him. God's Word makes this very clear:

> No one who abides in him keeps on sinning; no one who keeps on sinning has either seen him or known him. Little children, let no one deceive you. Whoever practices righteousness is righteous, as he is righteous. Whoever makes a practice of sinning is of the devil, for the devil has been sinning from the beginning. The reason the Son of God appeared was to destroy the works of the devil.

No one born of God makes a practice of sinning, for God's seed abides in him; and he cannot keep on sinning, because he has been born of God. By this it is evident who are the children of God, and who are the children of the devil: whoever does not practice righteousness is not of God, nor is the one who does not love his brother.

—1 John 3:6–10, esv

Notice that we're told to practice righteousness—not *self*-righteousness! Again, it's not our power, efforts, or merit that determines our righteousness. It's the blood of Jesus Christ. We simply live as men and women who have been reborn and renewed, stripped of our old default settings and reprogrammed with divine directions. We're instructed, "Since we have these promises, beloved, let us cleanse ourselves from every defilement of body and spirit, bringing holiness to completion in the fear of God" (2 Cor. 7:1, esv).

When others see us honoring God in how we live, work, act, relate, talk, walk, love, serve, lead, breathe, and smile, they will be drawn to know Him too! "Strive for peace with everyone, and for the holiness without which no one will see the Lord" (Heb. 12:14, esv). We are a royal priesthood, a holy nation, a chosen race, a people possessed by God, vessels chosen for His good works! We are called to proclaim "the excellencies of him who called you out of darkness into his marvelous light" (1 Pet. 2:9, esv).

As we begin to thrive, we grow and mature in our faith, entrusted with more responsibilities, resources, and rewards. That's what I've been telling people for my entire ministry, both during the pandemic and long before. You see, thriving is really quite simple. All you have to do is...

Walk like Enoch.

Obey like Noah.

Believe like Abraham.

Dig like Isaac.

Wrestle like Jacob.

Dress like Joseph.

Stretch like Moses.

Conquer like Joshua.

Come back like Samson.

Lead like Deborah.

Dance like David.

Judge like Solomon.

Confront like Elijah.

Plow like Elisha.

Pray like Daniel.

Weep like Jeremiah.

Worship like Mary.

Speak truth like John.

Climb up like Zacchaeus.

Shout like Bartimaeus.

Come out like Lazarus.

Give thanks like the leper.

Preach like Peter.

Serve like Stephen.

Break out like Silas.

Overcome like Paul.

Love like Jesus...

And change the world!

ALIVE TO THRIVE

As you've been doing at the end of each chapter, use the questions below to facilitate a time of reflection, renewal, and reactivation with the Lord. I encourage you to open yourself to God's Spirit and pray as the psalmist prayed for God to search your heart. After you've considered what it means for you to live a Christ-honoring life, spend a few minutes in prayerful conversation, using the starter provided or words of your own.

1. How do some of your passions and favorite things cause you to praise, worship, and honor God? How do some of your pursuits become idolatrous obstacles to honoring Him?

2. What's your definition of a Christ-honoring life? How is it different than simply giving an honorary acknowledgment?

3. What areas of your life clearly align with your faith beliefs? What areas are still developing and need to be yielded to the Holy Spirit's power again?

Lord, I want to honor You with all that I have and all that I am! You alone are worthy of praise, glory, and honor. Thank You for the many ways You have shown

Your love to me, especially the greatest gift of all, Your Son, my Savior, Jesus Christ. May all that I do create a sweet aroma for those around me as it drifts to Your throne in heaven! Let my life become a living sacrifice as I give myself—in all areas of my life—to You and ask Your Spirit to empower me so that I may thrive for Your glory, now and forever. Amen.

Chapter 9

ALIVE TO THRIVE—REFUSE TO SETTLE FOR LESS THAN GOD'S BEST

Once we learn to thrive, we will be called to break through barriers and blaze new trails.

Growth never ceases when we are thriving in the power of the Holy Spirit!

I F YOU HAD told me a few years ago that I would one day produce films shown in national theaters, including one with a song nominated for an Academy Award, we would have enjoyed a good laugh together. I would have thanked you for your humor and perhaps felt a spark of curiosity ignite my willingness to do whatever the Lord wants me to do, including movie producing. Or if the person sharing this vision was someone I knew and trusted, someone like my friend Cindy Jacobs, an extraordinary woman of God who serves as one of the seven elders whom I consult for guidance, then I would have been just a little afraid.

After all, what did I know about movies? I like watching many of them and appreciate the mass appeal they have to entertain, inspire, and inform millions of viewers around the world. But in terms of my involvement in them, I had never considered movies to be under the umbrella of my ministry. But then I let

God take away my imaginary umbrella and pour His blessings over me in a rain of divinely appointed opportunities!

Because as it turned out, a few years ago my friend Cindy Jacobs *did* in fact give me a prophetic word revealing that God would soon be leading me into a new area of ministry. I've been walking with the Lord long enough to know that when someone I respect and trust shares a prophetic word, then I'd better listen. So a while later when I heard my phone ping and opened it to see a news story from my RSS feed entitled "Mom Prays Loudly, Dead Son Comes Back to Life," I felt the hair on the back of my neck stand up.

The Holy Spirit was on the move.

The article told how a teenaged boy named John Smith had been out with some friends on the frozen surface of Lake St. Louis when the ice broke. All three toppled into the icy waters. One friend struggled to swim and made it back to shore while another clung to a sizable chunk of ice. By the time a rescue crew arrived, however, John had been submerged below the lake's surface for more than fifteen minutes. After attempting CPR to no effect on his lifeless body, they rushed him to the nearest hospital, where trauma doctors tried once again to resuscitate John. Their efforts were also in vain, and by then the eighth-grader's heart had not been beating for forty-five minutes.

Then John's mother, Joyce, arrived and like any parent was emotionally wrecked to see her son's unresponsive body. But Joyce was a devoted Christian woman and fierce prayer warrior, so she immediately began begging the Lord to restore her son's life. Her prayer was loud, bold, and intense—and before anyone could object or try to lead her out of the room, John's heart began beating. After defying every trauma expert, medical precedent, and scientific prognosis, John Smith fully recovered and walked out of the hospital under his own power sixteen days later. It was a miracle, one that Joyce and her family credited to the power of the Holy Spirit answering Joyce's desperate prayer.

The story lingered in my mind and in my heart, and I ended up using it as an example in a sermon. From that sermon, I ended up miraculously meeting Joyce Smith herself and hearing her story firsthand. Without a doubt that experience left me awestruck! I immediately felt the Holy Spirit tell me to share Joyce's story about John's miracle with the world—as a movie. Now, if the Spirit had told me to use my connections to help Joyce write and publish a book, I would not have been surprised. I have a little experience in that arena and would've been happy to share what I know. But the Holy Spirit made it clear to me that her story should be more—not just a book but also a movie.

After talking it over with my wife and my team of elders, I approached my friend DeVon Franklin, already a successful Hollywood producer of films such as *Heaven Is for Real* and *Miracles from Heaven*. He found Joyce's story just as compelling as I did and agreed it had to be on the big screen. The rest, as they say, is history!

Even after the deal was done, Joyce was writing a book, and the film was being shot, though, I still had no idea how God would use *Breakthrough* to, well, break through so many barriers! Not only had we assembled a first-rate cast of successful actors, but when we released the film's trailer in December of 2018, it garnered more than thirty million hits in forty-eight hours, a record for views of any religiously themed movie in that short time span. When the film released in 2019, it received mostly positive reviews and touched thousands if not millions of lives.

While we didn't expect the film to receive any Academy Award nominations, we were all delightfully surprised when

"I'm Standing With You" from the film's soundtrack was nominated. Performed by our film's star, Chrissy Metz, an Emmy-nominated breakout from the hit drama *This Is Us*, the song expressed so much of the powerful message behind the story. Seeing Chrissy perform on stage at the Dolby Theatre in Los Angeles for the 92nd Academy Awards brought tears to my eyes. Once again I marveled at how God works in ways beyond anything we can imagine when we're thriving in the power of the Holy Spirit.

BEYOND YOUR ZONE

I shouldn't have been surprised, really, that I ended up doing something so unexpected, because God's vision is always bigger than our own. When you're living a holy, healed, healthy, happy, humble, hungry, honoring life, you will be called to thrive outside your comfort zone. I'm talking *when* not *if* because God always has a bigger plan for our lives than we imagine for ourselves. Based on what we see in the Bible, most of the people God chose to advance His kingdom didn't aspire to greatness but simply remained willing and able to serve in whatever capacity the Lord called them to serve.

Many of them protested or made excuses—just ask Abraham or Jacob, Moses or Gideon, Naomi or Rahab. Others faced obstacles that appeared impossible to overcome based on human perception and earthly resources, including Noah, Joseph, Joshua, Jeremiah, and Ruth. One of my favorite examples, however, never questioned, wavered, or doubted God's ability to use him according to His infinite wisdom, limitless power, and divine will.

David was always willing to trust God for the next step, which is essential for thriving in the power of God's Spirit. As the shepherd king discovered, trusting God often requires ignoring the advice, opinions, and counsel of other people. But thrivers, those people whose spirits have been awakened by their anointing, aren't afraid to disrupt existing systems or traditional paradigms. Sometimes drastically altering or destroying a system or structure already in place is exactly what God wants us to do. If I had refused to persevere in producing movies when I hit the first obstacle, then I wouldn't have been obedient to what God asked me to do.

Returning to David's showdown with Goliath, we see that thrivers do not permit anyone or anything, no matter how large or threatening or powerful, to occupy their praise. You'll recall that the Philistines gathered their army and occupied Sokoh in Judah (1 Sam. 17:1), and that Judah means "praise." It cannot be repeated often enough that the enemy always wants to occupy your praise—through distraction, intimidation, diversion, conflict, crisis, or whatever it takes. So many people have struggled to praise God during the turmoil of recent events, but they're forgetting that this is exactly what the enemy wants us to do!

The devil will use anything and everything to derail your faith. He begins to defeat you the moment he takes hold of your worship. If he can take away your willingness to praise God, then the spiritual warfare will tilt in his favor. The enemies of truth, love, grace, and hope always come after your worship first. It's the same as a terrorist's first strike at the source of your power, fuel, and motivation. So cherishing, guarding, and practicing your praise must be a priority in order for you to thrive.

Do not permit failure to occupy your praise.

Do not permit fear to occupy your praise.

Do not permit anxiety to occupy your praise.

If I were a betting man, I would wager that the enemy attempted to occupy your Judah during the pandemic, the economic fluctuation, and all the civil unrest in the recent past. So if you have not already, I dare you to say, "Get out of my Judah! You cannot occupy my praise!" Claim the truth expressed by the psalmist: "The Lord is enthroned in the praises of His people." (See Psalm 22:3).

The Bible does not require you to be happy in order to praise God. The Bible does not require you to be smiling and joyful in order to praise the Lord God Almighty, Creator of heaven and earth. As a matter of fact, sometimes you must choose to praise while you're crying. Sometimes you praise while you're wounded. Sometimes you praise while you're hurting. Sometimes you're aching and you still have your praise.

In his poetic songs David often chose to praise God despite how he felt and everything going on around him. He basically said, "I'm broken, I'm wounded, I'm at the bottom of the pit, but I will not refuse from praising you." If we want to thrive, we must choose to praise with the same fierce determination. Don't let the devil steal your worship! Don't allow any obstacle to occupy your praise!

TESTIMONY TRUMPS TITLE

People thriving in the power of the Holy Spirit are not intimidated by titles—they're motivated by testimony. When David followed his father's instructions to take his brothers food and supplies on the battlefront, he could not have anticipated what he was about to face. Standing so many feet taller than anyone else, Goliath, however, could not be missed. In fact, his name was synonymous with the way he's identified in Scripture: "A champion named Goliath, who was from Gath, came out of the Philistine camp" (1 Sam. 17:4).

What a perfectly concise introduction! Notice that he's described as a champion named Goliath, not Goliath who was known to be a champion or soldier or Gathite (or whatever they called natives of Gath) or Philistine, although those are all included in his summary here. No, he is a champion named Goliath. Not an amateur, not a newbie at his first rodeo. Not a novice or even a veteran, but a champion. He held the title, wore the belt, and deserved the prize.

Yes, Goliath had a title. But David had a testimony.

Thrivers are not intimidated by titles. Thrivers are fueled by their trust in God and who the Lord has made them to be. We need people to stop caring about their titles and start becoming obsessed about their testimonies. It doesn't matter if you're the GOAT if you don't know the Lamb!

The Bible doesn't say we overcome by the blood of the Lamb and our title. It doesn't tell us that we have to be the greatest of all time at something before we invite the Holy Spirit into our lives. The Bible says we overcome by the blood of the Lamb and the *word of our testimony*! (See Revelation 12:11).

If you want to thrive, it's time to stop being obsessed with titles. Become enamored by the power of sharing a grace-fueled, faith-sustained testimony about the living God and the power of His Spirit at work in your life! When you have an up-to-the-minute testimony, you can overcome any old title.

Eventually your testimony will come in conflict with someone's title. We must all face Goliath. In boxing and UFC, you can't win the title unless you defeat the reigning champion. Some people want the spotlight when all they fought were no-name, untested, unproven amateurs, but when God permits a champion to stand in your way, it means it's time for the championship bout.

In other words, you can't be a champion unless you defeat a champion.

Thrivers rely on their testimony to fight for the championship.

If you're presently satisfied with second place, third place, or amateur status, then don't fight Goliath. You can continue to survive this way, but you will never thrive. Because if you want the prize, if you want to reign, if you want all God has for you, if you want to live life and life abundantly, if you want overflow and exceedingly abundant blessings above all, if you want to change the world, you must be willing to fight the fights others are not willing to fight.

Thrivers don't walk away from prophetic confrontations.

Thrivers are not afraid to tell the truth. Thrivers are not afraid to rebuke devils and cast out demons. Why? Because we can! Because we're called to thrive in the power of the Holy Spirit!

> God is looking for thrivers, the spiritual champions who dare stand up for righteousness.
>
> God is looking for thrivers, His champions who dare fight for justice.
>
> God is looking for thrivers, faith champions who dare face the giant and say, "You will not defeat my family, you will not intimidate my destiny, you will not prevent me from thriving."

Through the work Christ did on the cross, we are already spiritual champions with unlimited strength, stamina, and power. We're called more than conquerors (Rom. 8:37) and assured that if God is for us, who can be against us (Rom. 8:31).

God created you to do more than settle for surviving.

God created you to thrive.

SIZE MATTERS

People who thrive have usually faced a giant or two. If you walk by faith for very long, there comes a time in your life when an intimidating, overbearing, behemoth, mammoth, *mucho grande* giant shows up, often unexpectedly. We're told that Goliath was "six cubits and a span" (1 Sam. 17:4), and that's no trivial detail. Size and height matters when you're fighting battles of faith.

Our giants pop up in the forms of a problem, bad news, a scary diagnosis, financial calamity, marital strife, temptation, addiction, secret sin, and anything else that stops us in our tracks. No matter how and when our giant shows up, at the time it represents the biggest challenge of our lives.

Permit me to illustrate. If I stand behind someone way taller than me, then you cannot see me. This is the devil's objective: to obstruct others' ability to see Christ in you, with you, and through you. If the enemy can hide you behind a giant obstacle, then he disables your testimony, undermines your anointing, bruises your purpose, and hinders your destiny.

Not only that! The enemy also sends a giant to block your path so you're temporarily unable to see what's ahead of you. Hell is well aware that what's in front of you is greater than what's behind you. The enemy hopes you will lose focus on where you're headed and become distracted, disoriented, and discouraged. He doesn't want you to see the glory on the other side.

Here's the thing: the size of your giant is directly proportional to the size of your blessing!

Goliath was big.

Goliath was overbearing.

Goliath was intimidating.

Goliath was ginormous.

Yet Goliath made David famous.

Goliath expanded David's testimony.

Goliath catapulted David to prophetic stardom.

Defeating Goliath made David a thriver!

I'm convinced the size of the obstruction speaks to the size of the overflow, your imminent advancement. If something big stands in your way, it's only because you're about to step into something amazing! Please understand that giants come to block your view and obstruct your vision. The bigger the future God has for you, the bigger the giant that hell sends your way.

So no matter what you're facing or how uncertain, unprepared, or unequipped you may feel about the battlefield where God is calling you to advance, don't forget that big problems mean big promises. Big battles lead to big conquests. Big adversity means big accomplishment. As you transition from surviving to thriving, remember that no matter how big, how loud, how intrusive, how overbearing, or how tall a giant may be, by the power of the Spirit and in Jesus' name, that giant is about to fall! And the bigger they are, the harder they fall!

Rather than complaining, worrying, stressing, despairing, or attempting to control circumstances when giants appear, thank God for what's about to happen. There are giants we must conquer in order to move forward and take the next steps God wants us to take. Your future is based on what you're willing to face today. When a giant looms and sends you wondering why God allowed such an obstacle to fall in your path, trust that He will catapult you over that giant and into greatness.

Your heavenly ordained purpose will always be greater than

any hell-orchestrated problem! What's inside of you is greater than everything outside of you! Giants have the size, but you have the Spirit! They have the height, but you have the Holy!

THE TRUTH ABOUT LIES

The enemy's strategy is one of psychological warfare, false propaganda, and fear-inducing intimidation. More powerful than what he does is what he says. Unless you live by grace through faith, in holiness, the enemy's words will dismay and terrify you. But here's the thing: you must remember that when he speaks, he speaks in his native language of lies, for he is a liar and the father of all lies (John 8:44).

Forgive me for just telling the bald truth, but the devil is a flat-out liar! This is not just my opinion but the eternal truth of God's Word. The devil loves getting you to ruminate on events, conversations, false assumptions, and inaccurate conclusions. He loves distorting truth by tweaking it ever so slightly that you think he might be right. But, my friend, the devil lies—always!

He lies when he says you are not going to heaven.

He lies when he says your family will not be saved.

He lies when he says God doesn't listen to you.

He lies when he says you're never going to be happy.

He lies when he says you're never going to be holy.

He lies when he says you're never going to be healed.

He lies when he says you're never going to see your dream come true.

So how do you overcome his lies? With the truth from God's Word! Repeat after me and say the truth out loud:

I am saved (John 3:16).

My family will be saved (Acts 16:31).

God listens and answers (Jer. 33:3).

By the way, you perpetuate the enemy's lies when you jump to worst-case scenarios and give in to defeat before the battle is over.

You repeat the lie when you say that your child is an alcoholic.

You repeat the lie when you say you're never going to make it.

You repeat the lie when you say this sickness will be the end of you.

You repeat the lie when you say you're always going to live paycheck to paycheck.

You repeat the lie when you say you will never be free, you will never be happy, you will never be holy.

God wants you to thrive so that you will never bow down to the enemy's tactics of intimidation. Mind games are from the pit of hell. Jesus has already won—game, set, match!

Thrivers dwell on the truth of God's Word and immediately close any opening where the enemy seeks a foothold. God's promises power our positivity! He gives us the strategy for keeping our minds focused on truth: "Finally, brothers and sisters, whatever is true, whatever is noble, whatever is right, whatever is pure, whatever is lovely, whatever is admirable—if anything is excellent or praiseworthy—think about such things" (Phil. 4:8).

SERVE AND DELIVER

If you want to thrive, then you love to serve. And serving means obeying the Spirit and doing what God asks you to do, what needs doing in the moment, not what you're in the mood to do or want others to see you doing. David's family forced him into the role of errand boy delivering snacks, not that of a soldier sent to fight giants.

> Now David was the son of an Ephrathite named Jesse, who was from Bethlehem in Judah. Jesse had eight sons, and in Saul's time he was very old. Jesse's three oldest sons had followed Saul to the war: The firstborn was Eliab; the second, Abinadab; and the third, Shammah. David was the youngest. The three oldest followed Saul, but David went back and forth from Saul to tend his father's sheep at Bethlehem.
>
> For forty days the Philistine came forward every morning and evening and took his stand. Now Jesse said to his son David, "Take this ephah of roasted grain and these ten loaves of bread for your brothers and hurry to their camp. Take along these ten cheeses to the commander of their unit. See how your brothers are and bring back some assurance from them. They are with Saul and all the men of Israel in the Valley of Elah, fighting against the Philistines."
>
> —1 SAMUEL 17:12–19

David wasn't there to fight Goliath. He didn't go down to make a name for himself or appear on the BBC (Bethlehem Broadcast Company). He wasn't delivering weapons or vital information about the enemy. He wasn't a reinforcement sent so his brothers or other soldiers could rest. *David came to serve cheese sandwiches.* Don't you love it? That's the reason David happened to be on the front line and ended up fighting Goliath—because David was willing to serve, and in a way that wasn't dangerous, dramatic, glamorous, or important. Soldiers need to eat, and David's father, Jesse, had food to send his sons on the front line, and that food had to be delivered. David didn't whine or complain or refuse to go until there was a more significant reason. He went to deliver bread and cheese, a party platter from Panera!

God is not looking for superstars that seek the limelight; He is looking for a bunch of shepherds willing to serve cheese sandwiches. If you can serve those on the front line, then you qualify for the championship fight. We can't defeat the giant until we serve those already in battle.

Do you want victory over your giant?

Find someone facing a similar giant and serve them.

We're told, "As each has received a gift, use it to serve one another, as good stewards of God's varied grace" (1 Pet. 4:10, ESV). Serve that person fighting cancer, the couple fighting for their marriage, the person battling his or her addiction. Serve what others need that you have right now.

Thrivers help others be survivors.

NOW BEFORE NEXT

Thrivers also take care of the now before they step into the next. Notice that David didn't neglect his responsibilities as a shepherd before he left for the battlefront: "Early in the morning David left the flock in the care of a shepherd, loaded up and set out, as Jesse had directed. He reached the camp as the army was going out to its battle positions, shouting the war cry" (1 Sam. 17:20).

David left the flock in the care of a shepherd. Knowing he already had a responsibility, he did not abandon it. When you're facing your giant, show God that you will honor your responsibilities before you embrace your opportunities. Let's say you're asking the Lord for a new house; He's asking you what you're doing with the home you have now. You want to get a new car for safer, more reliable transportation, but God asks you how you have stewarded the vehicle you already have. You're asking God for a new job, but He's looking at the quality of your work in your old one.

You must take care of now before you receive the next.

You have to be faithful with the now before you are favored with the next!

Show God that you're not just jumping from season to season and opportunity to opportunity. You have to honor your current responsibilities before you embrace new opportunities! And you need to do it thoughtfully. David did not place his sheep in the hands of the auto mechanic. He did not place the sheep in the hands of a window washer. He placed a sheep in the hands of the shepherd! Only another shepherd knows how to fight off bears and lions. Only another shepherd understands you must go after a sheep that strays from the flock. Only another shepherd knows where to find the green pastures and still waters.

Thrivers stay in the now on their way to the next.

DON'T FORGET TO REMEMBER

Finally, thrivers remember where they've been in order to remove obstacles to where they're going. David recalled, "The LORD who rescued me from the claws of the lion and the bear will rescue me from this Philistine!" (1 Sam. 17:37, NLT). David knew that God did it before and He would do it again!

Thriving in the power of the Holy Spirit requires remembering your miracles along the way. Never forget to remember where God has brought you out of! I can't help but wonder if it took the Israelites forty years to find the Promised Land because they had spiritual amnesia! Time and time again they were told, "Be careful not to forget the LORD, who rescued you from slavery in the land of Egypt" (Deut. 6:12, NLT).

Don't forget what that place felt like, looked like, smelled like, tasted like, sounded like. Don't lose sight of where you still might be if not for the Lord's rescue. Again, the children of Israel were cautioned to remember the stark contrast between where they used to be and where they were going:

> Do not forget that he led you through the great and terrifying wilderness with its poisonous snakes and scorpions, where it was so hot and dry. He gave you water from the rock! He fed you with manna in the wilderness, a food unknown to your ancestors. He did this to humble you and test you for your own good. He did all this so you would never say to yourself, "I have achieved this wealth with my own strength and energy."
> —DEUTERONOMY 8:15–17, NLT

The apostle Paul reminded those who knew him to "remember my chains" (Col. 4:18). Most of all, however, he didn't want anyone to forget the full work of Jesus Christ on the cross! Jesus Himself provided us with such a powerful reminder in what we now call the Lord's Supper: "This is my body, which is given for you. Do this in remembrance of me" (1 Cor. 11:24, NLT).

And why do we remember? Because it reminds us of the power, strength, stamina, hope, faith, joy, peace, and resources within our access. Simply stated, God did it before and He will do it again!

> The same God that blessed Abraham is ready to bless you.
>
> The same God that exchanged a rocky pillow with heaven's ladder for Jacob is ready to take you from the hard place to the high place.
>
> The same God that made Joseph's dream a reality is ready to make yours come true!
>
> The same God that placed His DNA on the blind man is ready to open your eyes to His glory!
>
> The same God that filled the Upper Room with the Holy Spirit is ready to fill your life with the same Spirit that raised Jesus from the dead!

Because if He did it before, He will do it again!

Get ready to defeat the enemy of your God-ordained destiny and purpose, experience your greatest breakthrough, and step into a season of fulfillment and favor, because God knows how to help you do what must be done! When young John Smith's lifeless, nearly frozen body lay on a hospital bed and his mother, Joyce, walked in and faced every parent's worst nightmare, Joyce knew that God had the power to restore her son's life. She prayed, "I believe in a God who can do miracles!

Holy Spirit, I need you right now to come and breathe life back into my son!"

You have the same source of miraculous power inside you, my friend. The same faith that fueled David's impossible victory over Goliath. The same faith that restored the life of Joyce Smith's son. You have everything you need to thrive!

You have a faith that moves mountains.

You have a shout that brings down walls.

You have joy that cannot be explained.

You have a peace that passes all understanding.

You have a grace that is sufficient.

You have an anointing that destroys the yoke.

You have a gift that cannot be revoked.

You have a destiny that cannot be stopped.

You have a purpose that will be fulfilled.

You have a love that expels all fear.

You have mercies that are new every morning.

You have the strength of the Father, the grace of the Son, and the anointing of the Holy Spirit!

ALIVE TO THRIVE

As you consider what it means for you to thrive in the power of the Holy Spirit, use these questions below to guide you. Review the qualities that thrivers, from King David to Joyce Smith, have in common and consider the areas you want to surrender before the Lord. Then, if needed, use the prayer provided to get your conversation with God started before sharing your heart with Him.

1. When has God recently called you to move out of your comfort zone in order to thrive? How did He guide you and provide direction as you moved forward in obedience?

2. What are the giants looming before you right now? What are the rewards waiting on you when you trust God to help you overcome these giants? What's the most important truth you must remember as you go into battle?

3. What are the victories, triumphs, rescues, and provisions God wants you to remember as you move forward to face your giants? What prevents you from resting in the fact that God has done it before and will do it again?

Heavenly Father, thank You for creating me the way You've made me. I'm so grateful for the many ways You have already empowered and equipped me to thrive, and I praise You and thank You for where You're leading me next. Help me to not lose sight of my now even as I move into Your next. May I always seek to put You first, never myself or Your blessings, as I walk by faith and champion Your kingdom! Amen.

Chapter 10

SYSTEM UPGRADE—DEVELOP THE NEXT GENERATION

When you thrive by God's power,
you create an epic legacy that endures.

Thrivers store up treasure in heaven to secure an
eternal inheritance for future generations.

C HANGE EITHER FORCES us to survive or reveals an opportunity for us to thrive.

While change of any kind is rarely easy, it's often positive, necessary, and inevitable. In the tech world, programmers, engineers, and analysts rely on new discoveries, more efficient methods, and system upgrades to improve security, speed, and operational integrity. Upgrades prevent viruses and patch glitches that were overlooked in previous versions. They increase size capacity, provide cloud accessibility, and add new layers of protection against hacking, file corruption, and identity theft. This explains why our smartphones require updating regularly, along with laptops, tablets, and other programmable devices.

Nonetheless, I confess I'm often just as frustrated by system upgrades as anyone else. Though I pride myself on being a tech early adapter, I've discovered that technology now advances faster than I can keep up. No sooner have I grown accustomed to one operating system before it's time for another software update. Just when I've customized my screens the way I want them, new "improved" graphics rearrange my orderly apps. I haven't had to resort to asking my kids—or heaven forbid, my *grandkids*—for help yet in operating my phone or smart appliances, but I fear those days might come sooner than I think.

At the end of the day I'm not intimidated by change, though, because I know it's necessary for growth. Whether we're talking about technology, relationships, or ministry methods, change prevents stagnation, resignation, and overfamiliarity. God constantly refines us, prunes us, and prepares us for what we're called to do next. Following the voice of His Spirit and relying on His power enables us to embrace change without fear, trusting that our growing pains, no matter how severe, will draw us closer to God and enable us to serve His kingdom with greater impact.

Among the many lessons learned from the global pandemic and its collateral damage we realized how many everyday "necessities" are really luxuries. We realized how many blessings we take for granted or have gradually felt entitled to enjoy all the time, including our physical and mental health, our employment and finances, our families and homes, transportation and food. We accepted that our world was changing before our very eyes, leaving us with choices to make about what we truly believe and whom we're willing to trust.

When we grow too accustomed to anything, we face the temptation to overlook it or take it for granted over time. This includes our spiritual development and faith in God. We settle into ruts and grow lax about our personal discipline and lifestyle habits. We sacrifice time set aside to pray, worship, read the Word, and listen to the Holy Spirit. We let frantic, frenetic busyness consume our traumatized psyches and exhausted bodies. We surf and scroll on our phones instead of unplugging and relating with our loved ones face to face.

Recent dramatic changes in our world, however, forced us out of those comfortable routines. They forced us to take a long, hard look at who we are, what we believe, how we treat each other, what we want for this world, and what we want for our children and our children's children. We've been reminded that an important part of thriving is preparing and developing the next generations who will come behind us.

USE IT OR LOSE IT

In the corporate world, succession plans are essential for making transitions from leader to leader and team member to team member as smooth, seamless, and stable as possible. Large organizations, institutions, and even ministries and churches know that people come and go. Sometimes this is expected, and at other times people leave for reasons that were not planned. They don't want to rely on individuals and specific personalities to sustain growth and productivity. I know of some businesses in which every employee cultivates others within the company to replace them. They take the view that no one is indispensable, not even founders and CEOs, so everyone must commit to keeping the corporate mission alive no matter the changes.

Fundamentally it's a generational principle we see in Scripture, although with much more than financial profits at stake. God calls us to be good stewards of all we're entrusted with, for His purposes and not our own. This means we are blessed to be a blessing, conduits of grace, and conductors of generosity. When we focus on our own profitability, we become hoarders and lose sight of God as the source of everything in our lives. We hold tightly to what we have and slip into old mindsets that have us believing we can control the changes in our lives.

Jesus confronted this mindset in many different ways throughout His ministry on earth. In fact, every time I drive by a new warehouse filled with storage units for rent, I can't help but think of one parable Christ told in particular:

> The ground of a certain rich man yielded an abundant harvest. He thought to himself, "What shall I do? I have no place to store my crops."
>
> Then he said, "This is what I'll do. I will tear down my barns and build bigger ones, and there I will store my surplus grain. And I'll say to myself, 'You have plenty of grain laid up for many years. Take life easy; eat, drink and be merry.'"
>
> But God said to him, "You fool! This very night your life will be demanded from you. Then who will get what you have prepared for yourself?"
>
> This is how it will be with whoever stores up things for themselves but is not rich toward God.
>
> —Luke 12:16–21

This rich man, whom God Himself calls a fool, became shortsighted and lost his understanding of why we're given abundant harvests. The answer, of course, emerges in another parable Jesus told, the one about the master of the household going away and leaving his servants in charge of his resources (Matt. 25:14–30). The first servant invested his five talents, or bags of gold as some modern translations render it, and doubled his original capital. The second servant did the same with the two talents he had been given, doubling the investment. When the master returned, he told each of them, "Well done, good and faithful servant! You have been faithful with a few things; I will put you in charge of many things. Come and share your master's happiness!" (Matt. 25:21).

The third servant, however, blew it big time. He had taken his one talent and buried it in the ground. He hadn't lost it, which he considered his priority, but he had played it safe and risked nothing. This servant allowed his fear to overwhelm his faith, afraid of losing the talent he had been given and displeasing his master. When his master returned, though, the result was much worse than if the servant had invested and lost the talent. The master was furious because his servant wasted the opportunity to thrive! This servant, whom the master called "wicked and lazy" (Matt. 25:26, NKJV), was so focused on surviving that he missed his moment to thrive! Consequently he had his talent taken away and entrusted to the first servant. "For whoever has will be given more, and they will have an abundance. Whoever does not have, even what they have will be taken from them" (Matt. 25:29).

Thrivers refuse to play it safe.

Thrivers embrace change rather than run from it.

Thrivers know that if they don't use it for eternity,
they'll lose it forever.

TREASURES IN HEAVEN

When you thrive by the power of the Holy Spirit, you are entrusted to invest all that God has given you. As a steward of all your resources, you commit to maximizing the eternal profitability for God's kingdom. The Lord always expects a return on His investments. While He wants His children to enjoy the abundance of gifts He gives, He wants our attitude to reflect His own gracious generosity. Simply put, the more He blesses us, the more He expects us to bless others. The more He gives us, the more He expects us to invest. We can accumulate, save, and hoard money and possessions on earth, but we can't take them with us.

Only when we store up treasures in heaven can we increase our eternal legacy.

Motivating our risks is a desire to invest in things that will outlast our time here on earth. We take to heart Jesus' question about our ultimate goal: "What good will it be for someone to gain the whole world, yet forfeit their soul? Or what can anyone give in exchange for their soul?" (Matt. 16:26). Those people intent on thriving and not merely surviving know that serving God and reflecting His goodness and glory is its own reward. As the psalmist explains, "Good will come to those who are generous and lend freely, who conduct their affairs with justice. Surely the righteous will never be shaken; they will be remembered forever" (Ps. 112:5–6).

Think about that for a moment: a righteous man will be remembered forever.

Practicing righteousness, living for and investing your resources in God's purposes, lasts forever. Now that's a legacy that endures! That's what thriving is all about. The endgame for thrivers is to leave a righteous legacy for future generations: "They share freely and give generously to those in need. Their good deeds will be remembered forever. They will have influence and honor" (Ps. 112:9, NLT).

Your investing, giving, and sharing is not necessarily about money. Your finances are just part of what you're called to invest because all of it belongs to the Lord. It's His, He gave it to you, and you return it to Him through your eternal investments. God's Word says, "You will be enriched in every way so that you can be generous on every occasion, and...your generosity will result in thanksgiving to God" (2 Cor. 9:11).

What are some other ways you can practice godly generosity besides giving money? I'm glad you asked. Let's consider four big categories in which we can thrive by giving: our time, our talent, our attention, and our treasure.

Time

While the old saying claims that time is money, I believe the time we're given on this earth is priceless. Money comes and goes, but our time is a finite commodity; once we spend today, it's gone. And we're not guaranteed tomorrow. The Lord knows how long He wants us to live, and we must invest the time we're given in what matters most. All of us are guilty of wasting this precious gift, but thrivers are mindful of time traps and instead try to invest in activities, events, and relationships with the greatest eternal impact. We can choose each day to spend time with God, to serve others as we're called, to meet someone else's need, and to bring joy, peace, and hope to those we encounter. Once we're thriving by God's power, our time is His.

Talent

Each of us has been given unique abilities, talents, and gifts. We each have diverse backgrounds, experiences, and opportunities. Using all your personal constructive resources can draw others to God like no one else can—that's why there's no one else like you! Embrace your identity in Christ so that you can keep your ego in check and resist temptations to make your own accomplishments your motivation. God has made you who you are for a reason—invest your personal talents in the lives of others in ways that will outlive any award, trophy, title, or achievement.

Attention

This gift is so obvious that it's easy to overlook. Every day, though, you interact with the people God has placed in your life—your family, your neighbors, coworkers and bosses, team members and clients, friends who share common interests, friends from church, even the people you may only see occasionally or one time such as sales reps, wait staff, baristas, store clerks, delivery drivers, and other service providers. While we've all had to learn new limits and guidelines for social conduct, including social distancing, mask-wearing in shared spaces, and limited physical contact, we can still engage with those around us and give them our undivided attention. We all have countless opportunities to show kindness, patience, respect, and encouragement to one another. Every time we meet someone, we reflect who God is without ever having to say a word.

Treasure

While money may top the list, treasure includes more than just what we give to the church, to ministries and nonprofits, and to worthy causes. Really, everything we have been given falls into this category: our jobs, our homes, our cars, our possessions, our savings, our attitudes about finances—our entire lifestyle. Too often we think about how little we can give and still leave more than enough for ourselves. Instead God calls us to give all we've got, to share generously with others the same way He shares His bounty of blessings with us. In fact, the Bible makes it clear that how we give to others directly affects what we ourselves receive from on high: "Give, and it will be given to you. A good measure, pressed down, shaken together and running over, will be poured into your lap. For with the measure you use, it will be measured to you" (Luke 6:38).

Generosity is a hallmark of every follower of Jesus who thrives!

Investing in eternal treasures is what our life here on earth is all about.

Your value is not about what you accumulate but about how much you give away!

AN ETERNAL INHERITANCE

Our stewardship includes our most precious blessing, our children and the younger generations following in our footsteps. Our children will inherit what we invest in our generation: "A good man leaves an inheritance to His children's children" (Prov. 13:22, ESV).

God empowers us to slay giants in order to move forward and attain the goal He has set for us. As we've seen, the battle belongs to the Lord, and we simply have to trust Him and seize the opportunities to thrive we've been given. We do this as torchbearers illuminating the future for our children and their children and all generations following us. Everything you and I do right now has a direct consequence on everyone behind us. We can set the table for them to thrive as well or create additional obstacles for them to overcome.

Thrivers are committed to fighting giants now to clear the path for their children later. Thrivers know that God has already conquered, that Christ enables us to be more than conquerors, and that the Holy Spirit empowers us to create an eternal legacy. Jesus Himself told us, "I have told you these things so that in me you may have peace. You will have suffering in this world. Be courageous! I have conquered the world" (John 16:33, CSB).

He has defeated death once and for all, and by His glorious power we are more than conquerors with Him—we are, in fact, coheirs with Christ in God's kingdom. Empowered by His Spirit, we know the battles we win allow us to steward the rewards entrusted to us. God told the Israelites, "Take possession of the land and settle in it, because I have given it to you to occupy" (Num. 33:53, NLT). The land we possess—perhaps literally, but more importantly, spiritually—will be inherited by our children. They will have to face the consequences of the battles we fight as well as the ones we choose to avoid.

Nonetheless, our children will not inherit our sins. Our children will inherit our blessings! We're assured, "I will pour my spirit upon thy seed, and my blessing upon thine offspring" (Isa. 44:3, KJV). God places us in our specific families for a reason. We have the ability to influence, mold, and mentor our children and grandchildren unlike anyone else in their lives (Acts 16:31). They inherit our blessings: "Blessed is the man that feareth the LORD, that delighteth greatly in his commandments. His seed shall be mighty upon earth: the generation of the upright shall be blessed" (Ps. 112:1–2, KJV).

Like the people of Israel we can rest in the knowledge that our children will never live in what God took us out of. The Israelites lived in bondage in Egypt until God heard their cries and answered their prayers. He liberated them from their captors, sustained them on their journey through the wilderness, and delivered them into the Promised Land. They no longer had to live under the oppression of the past: "But Moses told the people, 'Don't be afraid. Just stand still and watch the LORD rescue you today. The Egyptians you see today will never be seen again'" (Exod. 14:13, NLT).

We're not called to forget or deny or pretend that we were never in whatever our particular Egypt may have been. A key part of our spiritual legacy is our testimony, our story of how God has delivered us and empowered us to triumph over all the giants, obstacles, and oppressors in our life's journey. Passover is celebrated to this day as a time of recognizing the protection God granted His people when the angel of death descended during their captivity.

We're called to be storytellers who pass down the epic of faith from one generation to the next. "Tell your children about it, and let your children tell their children, and their children the next generation" (Joel 1:3, CSB). Through our words and deeds of redemption we create monuments to the Lord's power and goodness. "We will use these stones to build a memorial. In the future your children will ask you, 'What do these stones mean?'" (Josh. 4:6, NLT). The spoils of battle, the tools of survival, and the trophies of grace stand to remind us and our descendants of how far God has brought us.

Frequently in the Scriptures we're told that names carry this significance: "Then the LORD said to Joshua, 'Today I have rolled away the shame of your slavery in Egypt.' So that place has been called Gilgal to this day" (Josh. 5:9, NLT). You see, *Gilgal* sounds like the Hebrew word *galal,* meaning "to roll."[1]

Thrivers know that our rock of ages knows how to roll! God delivered His people not only from slavery but from the shame of slavery. He rolled away their shame by the same power He used to part the Red Sea. By this time, as our journey together between these pages concludes, if you only take away one truth from all that I've shared, then please remember this:

God has created you not merely to survive but to thrive!

WALLS BECOME BRIDGES

I understand that it's not always easy to believe this in the midst of trials, turmoil, and tantrums. One of the great concerns many people shared with me during the days of the pandemic resulted from their perception that their children's inheritance was in danger. With the virus running rampant, the economy causing financial distress, jobs being lost, and people protesting injustice, many of us have wondered if all we've worked for, all the giants we've slain, has been in vain. The answer is absolutely not!

Our children will walk upon the ruins of what we bring down in our generation.

Our walls will become our children's bridges.

God's Word is clear: "For thus says the Lord: 'Even the captives of the mighty shall be taken, and the prey of the tyrant be rescued, for I will contend with those who contend with you, and I will save your children" (Isa. 49:25, ESV). The battles we're fighting, both internally and externally, become the stepping-stones to thriving for future generations.

For those who love and serve the Lord, our legacy will endure. One of my favorite promises in Scripture assures us, "Once I was young, and now I am old. Yet I have never seen the godly abandoned or their children begging for bread" (Ps. 37:25, NLT). The God who provided manna in the desert for the children of Israel will provide bread for His children traversing the desert in the twenty-first century! Our children will never have to beg and will never be forsaken!

God created our offspring and all those we're privileged to influence with our lives for His specific purposes just as surely as He designed us for our divine destiny. Our children will be taught by the Lord, and great will be their peace: "All your children will be taught by the LORD, and great will be their peace" (Isa. 54:13). Our children are filled with divine purpose—a purpose that hell cannot stop! Remind them, and yourself, that God knew them before you did:

> You made all the delicate, inner parts of my body and knit me together in my mother's womb. Thank you for making me so wonderfully complex! Your workmanship is marvelous—how well I know it. You watched me as I was being formed in utter seclusion, as I was woven together in the dark of the womb. You saw me before I was born. Every day of my life was recorded in your book. Every moment was laid out before a single day had passed.
> —PSALM 139:13–16, NLT

Nothing is a mistake or error in judgment on God's part. No matter what you think you're lacking or worried your children may suffer, rest assured that God is in control.

READY, AIM, PRAISE HIM!

No matter how diligent your faith or how closely you walk with the Lord, sometimes battle fatigue catches up with us. When all the news you read, all the headlines you see, and all the sound bites you hear drip with the toxic fear of bad news and worse predictions, it's time to remember you're more than a one-stone believer. You may be tired by the battles you're fighting day after day, and still the giants seem to loom up ahead of you. You may be exhausted by what's required of you simply to keep your head above water and to hold on to the hands of your loved ones.

But take heart, my friend, because you've got everything you need to keep on thriving! We must conclude our exploration of what it means to thrive and not just survive where we began: with a young shepherd boy taking on the impossible. I cannot emphasize enough to you the sheer, unfathomable certainty present that day on the battle line between the Philistines and the Israelites. Goliath had won and he knew it. David's brothers knew it, the other soldiers knew it, and King Saul himself knew it. They were terrified and certain of their defeat.

David, on the other hand, was certain that the battle belonged to the Lord. He would not take no for an answer; he would not be dissuaded by the pitying looks and angry taunts; he would not be deterred by his lack of experience, training, or weaponry. But he had faith. David was certain that the Lord was with him. He knew that Goliath could not be allowed to continue mocking God and disparaging the faith of David's people. So after trying on Saul's armor and saying, "Thanks but no thanks," David did what he knew to do.

He recalled how God had helped him defeat bears and lions in order to protect his flock of sheep on the dark hillsides outside Bethlehem. David went with what he had: his shepherd's staff and his slingshot. The only things he used from his surroundings were the five smooth stones he gathered from the nearby brook as he prepared to confront the giant called Goliath.

Why *five*?

Why not just one?

It's simple: he prepared for more than just one fight!

Too often we fall into the trap of seeing ourselves as one-stone Christians. We think that yes, God has brought us through so many hard times before, but this time is different. Yes, He has empowered us to defeat some impossible giants along the way, but not the one in front of us now. Yes, the Lord has always provided what we've needed when we need it, but apparently not this time. If that sounds like thinking you struggle to overturn, then check your spirit, my friend, because you're equipped for more than one Goliath!

David had five stones but only needed one.

You have the limitless resources of the almighty God.

You have more than just one stone.

You're not anointed just to knock down one giant.

You have enough stones to knock down every giant that comes your way.

That giant in your family is coming down.

You have a stone for the giant in your health.

You have a stone for the giant in your finances.

You have a stone for the giant in your past, the giant in your present, and the giant in your future.

You have a stone for every giant that would dare rise up against your children and your children's children.

You should never be afraid to run out of stones.

Why? Because you know where to find the brook!

As long as you know where the brook is located, you will never run out of stones.

As long as you know that in the presence of God there is fullness of joy, there is grace, there is a mercy, and there is victory, you will never run out of stones.

God provides for each generation the necessary weapon to defeat darkness.

Jacob had a ladder.

Joseph had a robe.

Moses had a rod.

Joshua had a shout.

Gideon had a sword.

David had a stone.

Elijah had a mantle.

But what do we have? We have the name of Jesus.

As you thrive in the power of the Holy Spirit, I challenge you to prophesy before you fight. Speak into the darkness before you attack it. America's military strategy always includes the air force, with the strategic goal of attacking from the high places first in order to do as much damage as possible before the ground forces come in. Your biblically substantiated, Christ-centered, Spirit-empowered declaration is prophetically the air assault on your enemies!

David released a stone, but it was God who made certain that it landed on Goliath's forehead and penetrated his skull. David used his slingshot, and God made it a kill shot! Simply stated, your job is to release the stone God has placed in your hands. Let God determine where it lands! Stop worrying about what happens after you release it.

You're no longer in control after you release it. Your job is to take what God has provided, aim it, and release it. God's job is to direct it to its proper destination.

As you grow in your faith, as you experience more fully the power of the Holy Spirit, as you become more like Christ, your aim improves! You go from surviving to thriving to releasing the spiritual power inside you to advance God's kingdom outside you.

My prayer for you is that you will know the fullness of who you are, whom you serve, where you're going, and what you're doing. More simply put, to *thrive!* Because when you thrive, my friend, then you're right in the middle of God's purposes for your life. You're empowered by the Holy Spirit, and you're experiencing the joy, peace, and contentment that can only come from doing what you were made to do.

As you celebrate thriving in the power of the Lord, I can think of no better song of praise than Psalm 150:

> Praise the LORD! Praise God in his sanctuary; praise him
> in his mighty heaven! Praise him for his mighty works;
> praise his unequaled greatness! Praise him with a blast of
> the ram's horn; praise him with the lyre and harp! Praise
> him with the tambourine and dancing; praise him with
> strings and flutes! Praise him with a clash of cymbals;

praise him with loud clanging cymbals. Let everything that breathes sing praises to the LORD! Praise the LORD!
—PSALM 150:1–6, NLT

I wonder if David wrote that song after slaying Goliath. He certainly could have! And you will have your own psalms of praise to shout before the Lord as you no longer settle for surviving and instead experience the power of thriving. No matter where you are right now or what's going on around you, you can choose to praise God and thrive. Ready, aim, praise Him!

If you are breathing, then praise Him.

If you made it this far, then praise Him.

If you survived the storm, then praise Him.

If you overcame by the blood of the Lamb,
then praise Him.

If the Lord is your Shepherd, then praise Him.

If nothing can separate you from His love,
then praise Him.

If you are more than a conqueror, then praise Him.

If you're living a holy, healed, healthy, happy, humble, hungry, honoring life, then praise the Lord! Because you are no longer surviving—*you are thriving*!

ALIVE TO THRIVE

Congratulations on finishing the book and experiencing the joy of thriving! As you reflect on what you've learned and how God has spoken to you through these pages, use the questions below to help your assessment and direct you to the next steps. Then spend some time in prayer, using the one provided to help you get started or your own words. Moving forward, seek the Lord's will for how He wants you to serve next and to create an eternal legacy for future generations.

1. What's one of the significant points, biblical truths, or personal applications you will take away from reading this book? What stands out most to you or continues to linger?

2. How would you describe the spiritual legacy you want to leave for your children and the generations behind you? What needs to change in your life in order to store up these treasures in heaven?

3. How has God used your experience of reading this book to speak to you? What is the prophetic word you're sensing from the Holy Spirit? What next step can you take to move closer to this calling?

Lord, thank You for all the ways I've been challenged, stimulated, and encouraged by Your truths in these pages. Reveal more of Your will for my life so that I may move forward with confidence, overcoming any giants who get in the way, and advance Your kingdom according to my anointed purpose. I praise You and worship You for all the battles You have already empowered and equipped me to win to get to where I am now. Once again, I surrender my heart and my life to serve You, my King. May I continue to thrive by the power of Your Spirit in me! Amen.

Notes

CHAPTER 1

1. C. S. Lewis, *The Problem of Pain* (New York: Macmillan, 1973), 81.

CHAPTER 2

1. Johanna Mayer, "Science Diction: The Origin of the Word 'Quarantine,'" Science Friday, September 4, 2018, https://www.sciencefriday.com/articles/the-origin-of-the-word-quarantine/.
2. Bible Hub, s.v. *"ruach,"* accessed July 21, 2020, https://biblehub.com/hebrew/7307.htm.
3. Blue Letter Bible, s.v. *"pneuma,"* accessed July 21, 2020, https://www.blueletterbible.org/lang/lexicon/lexicon.cfm?t=kjv&strongs=g4151.

CHAPTER 4

1. Bible Gateway, "3 John 2: The Passion Translation," footnote, accessed July 21, 2020, https://www.biblegateway.com/passage/?search=3+John+2&version=TPT.

CHAPTER 5

1. Blue Letter Bible, s.v. *"makarios,"* accessed July 21, 2020, https://www.blueletterbible.org/lang/lexicon/lexicon.cfm?t=kjv&strongs=g3107.

CHAPTER 6

1. C. S. Lewis, *The Complete C. S. Lewis Signature Classics* (New York: HarperOne, 2002), 103.
2. Mark Oaks, "Filthy Rags Continued," The Bible Church Online, February 11, 2005, https://www.bibleword.org/wp/flithy-rags-continued/2645.

CHAPTER 7

1. Bible Hub, s.v. *"manna,"* accessed July 21, 2020, https://biblehub.com/greek/3131.htm.

CHAPTER 10

1. Bible Hub, s.v. *"galal,"* accessed July 21, 2020, https://biblehub.com/hebrew/1556.htm.

My FREE GIFT TO YOU

I'm so happy you read my book. I hope you go on to live a holy, healed, healthy, happy, humble, hungry, honoring life.

As a thank-you, I am offering you the e-book for *You Are Next...* for free!

To get this FREE GIFT, please go to:
www.SamuelRodriguezBooks.com/gift

—— God bless ——

Samuel Rodriguez